T0243195

PRAISE FOR VERN DAVENPORT AND
ACCELERATING GROWTH

"This book should be essential reading for any executive who wants to build a culture of execution in their company. The concepts Vern lays out are simple, but implementation is hard unless you have the right tools. *Accelerating Growth* provides both tools and inspiration to help you realize the true potential of your organization."

—Richard Blackburn, CEO, Azurity Pharmaceuticals

"In my eighth year as the Founder-CEO of a rapidly growing company, I began using the term 'frustration iceberg.' It was a simple way of continually referring to the endless opportunity that lay beneath the surface that we just couldn't quite figure out how to tap into. Yes, we were rapidly scaling but we *knew* we could scale faster. That is when we dedicated ourselves, our entire Founding, Executive and Senior Management Team to The Management System. I have learned a lot of things in my last ten years as a Female Founder CEO—many by luck, many by pure grit, trial, and error—but one thing I know for sure is The Management System works. This book lays out every step we took to drive The Management System into our organization. Eloquently written, it is your step-by-step guide to get you from where you are now to where your company is destined to be. If your team follows this book, this plan, this methodology—you will cross the chasm and tap into that unlimited potential. It won't be easy, as change never is, but I can promise you, it works!"

—Bethany Bray MRes, MBA; Founder and CEO, AutoCruitment

"Vern lays out what companies need to *grow with intent*. His proven system enables teams to develop, executive, and monitor business strategies in a continuously changing business environment."

–Faisal Mushtaq, Former CEO, Trueveris

"*Accelerating Growth* is a must read for any founder and/or CEO whose company is at an inflection point and struggling with financial, operational and strategic issues. Vern Davenport provides an easy-to-understand roadmap for implementing a new management paradigm that will revolutionize the way a company conducts its business. By uniting employees in vision, mission and purpose, helping them to better understand functional as well as individual roles and responsibilities, and, last but not least, providing a construct for delegation of authority, Vern's business tool, The Management System, enables companies to rapidly professionalize and scale."

–Ashton Poole, Partner, QHP Capital

"'Results' are the quintessential measure of success for a business. As a management team, it is always a challenge to isolate what truly matters most to drive optimal results. In each of the companies that I have brought The Management System to, the System has proven to be an invaluable tool to drive alignment, prioritize what matters most, and create an efficient, fact-based approach for relentless management focus—all of which directly yield results. The results produced each time have been mighty and allowed us to reach transformational goals."

–Amy Amick, CEO, Aspirion

"Business success often depends on a company's ability to be brilliant in the basics. The Management System is ideal for maintaining a spotlight on these few most important measures."

—Ben Clark, Customer Service Executive

"Now there is a powerful must-read book that really shows that Private Equity Investment is not just about the financial engineering of companies but can transform businesses into value-creation enterprises to the benefit of all stakeholders. Vern Davenport uses his wide business experience to show how The Management System—which is the essence of the book—works in practice and brings to life, through actual examples, a proven comprehensive methodology for company boards to employ as the path to great success."

—Gerry Brown, Chairman, G. Brown Associates

"*Accelerating Growth* presents a clear and important way of driving strategic growth. I have personally witnessed the power of the System and believe it is a differentiator for QHP and the companies they work with."

—Bob Greczyn, CEO Emeritus, Blue Cross and Blue Shield of North Carolina

"I often reflect on the years I have been in management, the countless hours I have spent in meetings and think, *If only I had read this book sooner.* This is a book to highlight, dogear, and read cover to cover."

—Jeanne Taylor Hecht, CEO and Chairwoman of the Board, Lexitas

"*Accelerating Growth* clearly and succinctly lays out the key elements of The Management System that have been at the heart of our growth journey for five years. The Management System itself drives alignment, transparency, and focus across an extended leadership team and in the course to the teams who report to those leaders. I am excited to see those concepts laid out in this book."

—Nick Dyer, Chairman of the Board and CEO, Catalyst Clinical Research

"Vern Davenport's careful and thorough work, *Accelerating Growth*, is truly groundbreaking. It provides a detailed path to scaled corporate growth and success through management structures and documented processes that are built to last. Key notions such as True North, From-To Chart, Alignment Sheets, and many more are combined into a comprehensive, coherent system that is efficient, effective, and easily made operational. Without any reservation whatsoever, I recommend this captivating and practical text for both an exhilarating educational read and a skill set that you will use for professional benefit."

—Sir Dennis Gillings, CBE, FMedSci; Chairman and CEO, GF Management

"I was most impressed by the depth and breadth covered by Vern. The text presents a complete management approach for an ambitious company aiming for growth and scale. Goals about education, delegation, and empowerment are aligned with detailed descriptions of compelling management tools. The book is instructive, rigorous, and practical. I recommend it as both an urgent read and an important study."

—Lady Mireille Gillings, PhD, Hon DSc; President, CEO, and Executive Chair, HUYABIO International

"I have applied and practiced The Management System in companies ranging from large and publicly traded to privately held and early stage. It always amazes me how the System unlocks the potential of employees at all levels of the organization, no matter how big or small. I have witnessed the C-level, as well as the front lines serving customers, embrace its principles to achieve amazing results."

—Matt Jenkins, Partner, QHP Capital

"A clearly differentiating aspect of The Management System is how it forces management teams to assign responsibility and drive account-ability to a single function. Whatever the metric—Revenue, EBITDA, the Order Book, Sales Pipeline, On-Time-In-Full delivery, Net Promoter Score—The Management System leaves nothing to doubt. Everyone on the team, and when fully implemented, the entire organi-zation knows *who is accountable*, and *exactly how that accountability will be measured* and tracked each month. This clarity unifies and energizes the team because each member is crystal clear about how their specific role and responsibility contribute to the whole."

—JV Wulf, Executive Chair, Spectra Medical Devices

"'You can only execute through your people.' *Accelerating Growth* takes the tools from Davenport's Management System and teaches readers how to put said tools into meaningful action. It's filled to the brim with insightful new ideas, robust illustrations, and an empow-ering focus on human centricity—especially in middle management. Absolutely worth the read."

—Alex Miller, CEO, Synergetics

"*Accelerating Growth* explains concepts and associated principles that any company can implement and adapt to accelerate and sustain success. Through relatable examples, Vern's engaging narrative uses real-world illustrations of companies at various stages to showcase the sustaining transformative effects of applying The Management System at key inflection points."

—Ed Seguine, Former CEO, Clinical Ink

"As an independent board director of ClinicalInk, I experienced firsthand how The Management System aligned the team, focused the work on the top impact areas, and accelerated performance. It truly works!"

—Diana L. Nole, EVP and GM, Nuance Healthcare Division

"*Accelerating Growth* expounds a revolutionary framework for companies and private equity partners to achieve transformational growth on a quest to True North."

—Eric Deyle, Global Co-Head, Eaton Partners, a Stifel Company

"As a founder, I've seen firsthand how The Management System has transformed our company, showing that when we combine forces, the result is greater than the sum of its parts. This approach has redistributed decision-making, empowering leaders at all levels and invigorating our middle management. Our collaboration with QHP is not just about investment—it's about jointly constructing a framework for growth and providing guidance while valuing our autonomy.

Embracing The Management System has revolutionized our approach, decentralizing decision-making and empowering middle management. This partnership, a beacon of Vern's wisdom on collaboration, has elevated our growth while honoring our founder-led spirit."

—Dr. Moby Kazmi, Co-Founder and President, Copilot

"Practical wisdom from an extraordinary business leader, and practical wisdom for driving explosive growth in any business. I've personally seen the business transformation unlocked by The Management System, and this book generously shares a detailed blueprint for others to follow. Unlike most business strategy books—grounded in philosophical jargon—this book provides a detailed blueprint for business transformation and explosive growth. I've had the privilege of seeing the installation and impact of The Management System firsthand, and *Accelerating Growth* generously shares a blueprint for unlocking transformation and explosive growth in your own business."

—Michael Burke, Google Sales Leader, Independent Director

"*Accelerating Growth* should be at the fingertips of every leader who is looking for a blueprint to drive clear accountability and rapid transformative results—and The Management System offers that blueprint. As a management consultant, I had the opportunity to put these concepts to work with several of the executive teams profiled in this book and they radically changed their odds of success leading transformations. Thank you, Vern, for sharing how The Management System works in practice and demystifying what it takes to drive outsized value in organizations."

—Allison Bailey, Senior Partner and Managing Director, Boston Consulting Group

"As a board observer and early investor alongside the QHP team, I've witnessed the power of The Management System in action. Through alignment around mission, vision, and values and full leadership buy-in on True North objectives, QHP and Management transformed Azurity from a sub-scale compounding kit business to a category-defining provider of innovative, high-quality medicines that serve underserved patients."

–Michael Barzyk, Global Head of Private Equity,
Allstate Investments

"In my unique position of having worked closely with Vern during The Management System's development at Misys and subsequently leading value creation in private equity for the past fifteen years, I have witnessed the evolution of these powerful concepts. Vern's book, *Accelerating Growth*, brilliantly applies this system to the dynamic landscape of private equity, and having seen its inception, I can attest to the profound impact it can have on improving company performance. This book is an invaluable resource for both management teams and private equity professionals looking to leverage its power in the increasingly competitive realm of private equity."

–Cory A. Eaves, Partner, Head of Portfolio Operations, BayPine

"*Accelerating Growth* presents the foundational principles for growing a business and articulates a management operating system with a set of tools and processes. The book clearly explains how to engage your people, achieve alignment and focus, and employ metrics that matter to ensure your company gets on track and sustains unprecedented growth."

–Jeff Kasher, PhD, Pharma Executive, Innovator, Board Member,
Mentor

"It is one thing to hear about The Management System, but quite another to see it in action. Working with Vern for years, I have experienced both. Straightforward in principle, The Management System puts businesses forward in practice."

—Patrick Jordan, Managing Partner, NovaQuest Capital Management

"The Management System detailed in Vern Davenport's book is nothing short of transformative. Its emphasis on simplicity and clarity provides a clear roadmap for success, ensuring that everyone is on the same page and aligned towards common goals. The nimbleness it encourages allows teams to adapt swiftly to challenges, staying ahead in today's dynamic business landscape. Its commitment to connectivity and inclusion truly sets it apart, fostering an environment where diverse voices are heard and valued, leading to unparalleled innovation and collaboration. If you're seeking a comprehensive approach to management that combines clarity, nimbleness, connectivity, and inclusion, this book is your indispensable guide."

—Frank Leo, Former Pharmaceutical Executive; Advisor, QHP Capital

"The Management System allowed for a true success story within Azurity Pharmaceuticals. Not only did The Management System integration provide clear granular guidelines for how to operate efficiently, but it also allowed an organization to demonstrate its true potential for growth and success. I live by and swear by The Management System in my everyday execution as I have seen the adoption of The Management System transform a company that operates well, into a company that operates flawlessly."

—Phillip Shilling, Vice President of Business Operations, Azurity

"The Management System was initially implemented at Azurity on the heels of QHP's investment, and then subsequently refreshed during each annual management offsite and at each major M&A integration. Accordingly, I've had a front row seat at over half a dozen such offsite sessions from multiple perspectives based on the role I happened to hold at the time—initially as a board member, then as CEO, and finally as Executive Chairperson.

The fascinating thing to me is that each time, I was learning and uncovering insights as much as my fellow colleagues who were participating for the first time. I've witnessed the implementation of alternative managerial approaches at many companies including start-ups, PE-backed portfolio companies, and publicly traded companies. What sets The Management System apart is an unmatched level of resulting clarity and alignment. Significantly more time and effort (and debate!) is invested upfront to get through difficult questions regarding objectives, roles, accountabilities, and operationalizing of the overall plan, which then pays dividends when it comes to effectively running a company. This entire experience results in a culture of execution wherein colleagues are inspired to collaborate and perform at levels not otherwise contemplated as possible."

–Amit Patel, Executive Chairperson, Azurity

"As a new executive joining an organization that had embraced The Management System already—it not only facilitated my onboarding but also provided support for where and how I could positively impact the business. With the combination of True North, Roles & Responsibilities, Tracking Sheets and red A3s, I was able to learn a lot about where the business was focused, how it was being operated, where it was ahead and behind versus target, and what the team had diagnosed as the root causes of challenges and the proposed areas of action. On day one, I was immediately able to engage with supporting those areas of the business, and their action plans—a massive accelerator of my learning and engaging.

As I established my role and looked at how I could best support the Operations unit with scaling, optimizing performance and removing friction in our delivery—I turned to The Management System and replicated it at a lower level in our operational organization. We repeated the whole exercise with middle management, and through the off-site discussions and resultant R&R documents, we resolved gaps and confusion in accountability and performance, locking in on the accountabilities and metrics that would allow us to continue to improve performance and support growth. As we established our monthly cadence of tracking-sheet and A3 review, the middle management recognized that they were now benefiting from the same approach their executives had been using to drive growth and loved that opportunity to benefit similarly in their current role. For me, it also helps them prepare for future executive engagements—another key benefit."

—Nik Morton, President and COO, Catalyst Clinical Research

ACCELERATING GROWTH

VERN
DAVENPORT

ACCELERATING GROWTH

A BLUEPRINT FOR
STRATEGIC TRANSFORMATION

Forbes | Books

Published by Forbes Books, Charleston, South Carolina.
An imprint of Advantage Media Group.

Forbes Books is a registered trademark, and the Forbes Books colophon is a trademark of Forbes Media, LLC.

Printed in the United States of America.

10 9 8 7 6 5 4 3 2 1

ISBN: 979-8-88750-343-1 (Hardcover)
ISBN: 979-8-88750-344-8 (eBook)

Library of Congress Control Number: 2024901149

Cover design by Matthew Morse.
Layout design by Megan Elger.

This custom publication is intended to provide accurate information and the opinions of the author in regard to the subject matter covered. It is sold with the understanding that the publisher, Forbes Books, is not engaged in rendering legal, financial, or professional services of any kind. If legal advice or other expert assistance is required, the reader is advised to seek the services of a competent professional.

Since 1917, Forbes has remained steadfast in its mission to serve as the defining voice of entrepreneurial capitalism. Forbes Books, launched in 2016 through a partnership with Advantage Media, furthers that aim by helping business and thought leaders bring their stories, passion, and knowledge to the forefront in custom books. Opinions expressed by Forbes Books authors are their own. To be considered for publication, please visit **books.Forbes.com**.

To my wife, Julie, who has been completely supportive not just through the process of writing this book but through my entire life journey.

CONTENTS

ACKNOWLEDGMENTS

FROM MY UPBRINGING, I could hardly imagine the professional career that I've had the opportunity to experience. There are many to thank who have both contributed to my career and also to what we now call The Management System.

To Steve Murphree (posthumously) who hired me right out of MBA school to IBM, which could not have been a better place to start a business career.

To Woody Stoke who was my branch manager at IBM and taught me more about managing and leading people than any other person in the business world.

The Management System would simply not be possible without my partnership with Ron Scarboro, who I had the fortune to hire as the CFO at Misys Healthcare. Ron became a true partner in the early days of the development of The System, and today remains one of the finest operational CFOs I've ever known. Ron is taking The Management System into depths of organizations that we did not even dream of when we worked together at Misys, with significant financial and operational acumen, and a commitment of discipline which are all now substantial elements of the system. Today he serves as CFO of one of our QHP investments, Azurity Pharmaceuticals. There, The Management System has completely transformed that family-run business into a true powerhouse in the 505 B2 pharmaceutical space.

Also, I need to acknowledge the many executives who have been part of the teams of the companies that I have led. Their own commitment to The Management System and to organizational success has clearly contributed to mine. I certainly cannot mention everyone's name, as they are just too numerous to do so, but I would like to call out a few: Ben Clark, Amy Amick, Faisal Mushtaq, Axel Granholm, Mike Etue, Mike Raymer, Kathy Twiddy, and Cary Eaves. In their own way, each provided great leadership and went on to great success and, in many cases, running their own companies.

As of today, QHP has thirteen companies in the portfolio. Each has adopted The Management System. I need to acknowledge the contribution of those CEOs and management teams, especially Nick Dyer at Catalyst Clinical Research and Ed Seguine at Clinical Ink. All are involved in the significant transformation of a business, in turn making a great contribution to the healthcare industry.

BRIDGING THE GAP BETWEEN PRESENT AND FUTURE

s your company at an inflection point? Do you see great potential for transformation and growth but don't know how to make it happen? Transformation is possible. Rapid, significant growth is possible. But you need a blueprint for getting there. To show you just how much potential there can be, let's look at two companies that my growth-oriented private equity firm, QHP Capital, partnered with to grow swiftly and dramatically: Azurity Pharmaceuticals and Catalyst Clinical Research. Azurity grew from $30 million in revenue and $5 million in EBITDA to over $500 million in revenue and $200 million in EBITDA in just five years. Likewise, Catalyst grew from a start-up with eighteen employees and $12 million in revenue into a leading oncology-focused clinical research organization with nine hundred employees and $150 million in revenue in just four years.

Your potential for transformation and growth is real, and you *can* make it happen.

What is the blueprint for this kind of success? How does QHP Capital achieve tremendous growth with the companies we work with? How can you do the same thing? The answer is not simply by securing financial investment. Money is only the starting point. Any investments in your company must be used intelligently and purposefully, or it will just be money down the drain. What you need is a proven methodology for getting your company from where it is now to where you dream of it being. At QHP, we call that methodology The Management System. Effective use of this system has driven the amazing growth I described above—and many other dramatic business transformations.

I first developed The Management System when I became CEO of Misys Healthcare. Misys had lost its way but had great potential. About a month into my tenure, I came into my office to find twelve thick white binders piled up on my conference table. I asked my assistant what they were, and she told me that they were my board books, the monthly reports from each of the company's business units. I picked up the first one and was greeted by seventy-five pages of dense narrative. Discouraged, I picked up the next one: a raft of spreadsheets. The twelve binders contained hundreds of pages of graphics and narratives—more than anyone could process in a year, let alone every month! I was astounded that anyone could run a company based on this tidal wave of information.

I asked my business unit leaders what they expected me to do with this mountain of information and how I could use it in any kind of practical way. I thought I'd gotten my message across, but the next month twelve *more* big white binders showed up in my office! At that point, I informed those leaders that if they felt the urge to give me another one of those binders next month, they might as well leave their letters of resignation on top of it.

But, of course, knowing what *not* to do is not the same as knowing what *to* do. I was fortunate to have worked for three great process-oriented, results-driven companies: IBM, Siemens Medical Solutions, and Kodak Health, where I learned Lean Six Sigma, Total Quality Management, and other process and transformation management approaches that provided a great foundation. But I didn't have specific tools that I could apply to developing the kind of system I felt was needed at Misys. What I was looking for was a system that would ensure that the organization was aligned and focused on the most important work that needed to be done—the work that was required to exceed our objectives for the year. And I needed a way to see if we were on track or not on track to accomplish those objectives along the way so that we could adjust accordingly. This all *sounds* simple enough, but if you're reading this book, you already know how hard it is to accomplish.

I asked my managers at Misys if anyone had experience with Lean Six Sigma. We worked with the Six Sigma core concepts—the powerful, practical ideas in Pascal Dennis's excellent book *Getting the Right Things Done*—and my own experience with company transformations to build a new management framework and deploy it. We called our new framework simply The Management System. I also hired Ron Scarboro (now CFO of Azurity Pharmaceuticals) as my CFO, and Ron was instrumental in filling out The Management System and operationalizing it. Using The Management System, Misys turned itself around in just twelve months, growing into an enterprise with $600 million in revenue and $92 million in operation profit.

That was the beginning of The Management System, and over the years my colleagues and I have continued to refine the system. If you follow it faithfully—as we do when we partner with companies at QHP—and make the system your own, you can transform your company into the one you know it can be and want it to be.

One of the reasons that The Management System works is because it takes a revolutionary approach. I'm a revolutionary change kind of guy, not an evolutionary one. At Misys Healthcare I felt I *had to be* revolutionary, because the need for change was so great. And that mindset is appropriate for companies that find themselves at an inflection point. Decision-making is hard. Being accountable for those decisions is even harder. Enabling others in your organization to make consequential decisions may be the hardest of all. But this approach demands all three of those things. In order for a company to grow, decision-making has to cascade down into the organization or the company will continue to grow slowly—or cease to grow at all.

Does The Management System really do what I'm claiming it does here? I'll let others who have worked with the system speak for it.

Richard Blackburn, CEO of Azurity, recognizes the way The Management System aligns a company's business and purpose:

> In order to grow, everyone in your organization needs clarity. We spent time as a leadership team to find a new clarity about our purpose, about what we do and don't do as a business. Inspired by Patrick Lencioni's book *The Advantage*, we also defined strategic anchors for the company—the critical factors that define business success for us. We asked ourselves Lencioni's key questions, including: *Why do we exist? What do we actually do? How will we succeed? How will we behave?* When you've got those things clear and everybody is aligned on the strategy, then you can have a very productive conversation about: *What are the most important things we need to do right now?* and *Who needs to*

do what? That's where The Management System comes in and proves invaluable—it gets people aligned on direction, priorities, and roles, and enables you to set the right metrics for success.

Another CEO emphasizes the clarity The Management System brings to doing the work necessary to grow a company:

> With The Management System, you start by defining all the roles and responsibilities within the company. In the old version of our company, everybody was pitching in, doing this, that, and the other thing. There were no clear definitions. And when you operate like that, important things can fall through the cracks because nobody knows who exactly is doing them. But with The Management System, you know exactly what everybody's doing. Everybody has their job defined—and in many cases redefined—so that their focus is on the right work necessary to grow the company. The system realigns your organization for success.

And finally, my fellow QHP Partner Ashton Poole, who has not only been a CEO himself but has also worked for other investment firms, describes why using The Management System differentiates our approach from that of other investors:

> Other investment firms are very KPI-driven. They have a ninety-day plan, they delineate the things that they expect the company to accomplish over that period and provide a kind of checklist for getting those things done. But that's not really a long-term strategy. QHP provides a framework that does many things for a company on an ongoing basis: establishing processes, defining roles and responsibilities, defining the right metrics and how to measure them, and so on. It's

a living, breathing, evolving plan led by company management and championed by the CEO. Engaging and empowering the whole company is really important to long-term success and growth. As the majority shareholders, QHP could be heavy-handed, telling a company, "*This* is what you're going to do. *This* is your ninety-day plan." But we use a very different approach. We educate, delegate, empower the organization, and help them to empower themselves, so they have the tools to perform at their best.

What Happens at an Inflection Point?

How can you tell when a company has reached an inflection point where things need to change? What are the attributes of such a company? At QHP, we see them as companies that have robust market opportunities—and management teams that are passionate about those markets—but are not realizing their full potential. There can be many reasons for this: a lack of capital to fuel the growth, a lack of talent to pursue the opportunity, a lack of process to scale the business, conservatism, lack of vision by the senior management team and the owners, or *all* these reasons. What appears to be common to all the companies QHP has partnered with is that they don't know how to get from where they are today to where they can realize the full potential they see for their business.

Companies at a growth inflection point, or at a point of transformational strategy shift, need to change significantly and quickly to capitalize on a market opportunity, reposition themselves competitively, or undertake a major merger or acquisition. We see various kinds of inflection points in the companies we work with, such as those that:

- Face multiple challenges and opportunities, compelling them to evolve and adapt rapidly

- Have evolving customer demands and increasing business uncertainty, so they need to be more responsive and agile

- Have limited resources and margin pressures, requiring them to be highly focused and highly efficient

- Need to ensure alignment and autonomy in decision-making, so they require tools and processes that ensure accountability

We do a significant amount of due diligence before we make an investment. We typically engage market consultants to do an independent evaluation of the market. We take into account the perspective of the company, its view of the market, and its ability to successfully sell in that market. We compare these inputs and produce an investment thesis that is evaluated and ultimately must be approved by our investment committee.

The target company also has its own projections that incorporate their views of the future expected growth of the company, assuming sufficient investment to fuel that growth. Those projections are called the management case, and our projections are called the investment case. The company "sells" us, as a private equity company, their five-year projection, and we invest on the basis of common expectations about the growth potential of the company.

So, at the time we make an investment, we have established the financial and operational status of the company and have aligned with the owners on its potential. In most cases, this represents an optimistic outlook for the company and a confident view of its ability to execute against this opportunity. We then document a variety of factors that create a picture of where the company is today and where we all believe it can be in five years.

For example, some of those elements for comparison are revenue, profitability, employees, products, and customers. I call this vision the From-To Chart. This chart frames the fundamental alignment between the company and our private equity firm. It's important that both QHP and the management team share the vision of the company's potential for growth. By the time we start working with a company, all of that has been established: we're committed to each other, and we're working in tandem. We have agreed that there is a great market opportunity to pursue. This is a critical point, because we can now start focusing on how we use The Management System together to execute against the potential we all see.

In many of the companies we partner with, decision-making is limited to a few individuals at the top: the founders, the CEO, and his/her small network of trusted leaders. Processes are suboptimized because they are completely dependent on a small group of critical people making all the important decisions. Knowledge of how the company works is not fully understood by the middle managers and the employee base, because they're not privy to what's going on in the company as a whole. Investments in key functions have suffered because cash has been totally controlled by those at the very top. As a result, key functions and processes are not robust enough to support rapid growth or a rapid shift in strategy. The business is dependent on specific people and relationships and not on good processes. This has become the bottleneck that limits the growth of the company.

You can only execute through your people, so at an inflection point, your middle managers need to be effective. This is the group that sits between the CEO (or the CEO and executives who are determining strategy) and the individual contributors that must execute the company's growth strategy. Growth requires applying systemic changes to that much larger group of middle managers. They are the ones who deploy the new strategy throughout the company. The Management System is designed to drive management acumen deep into the organization to avoid bureaucratic inertia. The Management System tool set can be used at all levels of the company as it grows, ensuring that change happens.

Chick-fil-A is not a QHP client; however, a lot of people eat there, including all of us at QHP, and they provide a great example of effectively driving management acumen deep into the organization, which is our goal as well. Every store is clean, the food is consistently good, and the service is outstanding. That's because they've got a middle management team with the ability to hire people, train people, and demand performance out of people that's consistent with corporate values. It doesn't matter if an employee has been there one day or ten years—you get the same great experience interacting with them. This is clearly the result of a focused, aligned, and committed middle management executive team.

We've used The Management System with both smaller and larger companies. Regardless of size, the key is the clarity of your strategy and the engagement of your middle management team, who then drive the strategy and engagement down into their own teams.

In smaller companies, you don't have nearly as much of a middle management team, if any at all, so all decisions of consequence are made by a few executives. But to scale a company and rapidly grow, you need to build a strong middle management team and a system that drives the efficient execution of the business into all levels of the company. The advantage of smaller companies is that they can usually implement and adjust to a new system more nimbly.

Large companies have that robust middle management layer, but the shift to moving faster and getting bigger can be more difficult among a larger group of people. The Management System tools can also be cascaded down through a large organization, driving efficiency and effectiveness across the organization.

The tool set is always the same, but the execution will be different for each company. There will be people in both large and small companies who are not comfortable working within a strong framework. With The Management System, you will be able to quickly identify people who aren't working well within the system and educate or replace them. In my experience, there is a "rule of thirds" about staffing for a transformation: you want one-third incumbents for stability, one-third promoted into new positions for enthusiasm and to get buy-in from the broader team, and another third brought in from the outside to fully inject the new approach into the organization.

Passionate and aware leaders at the top, who really care about growing the company, will eventually realize that their current way of working will not allow that growth to happen. What got the company to its current level of success will not be sufficient to achieve future objectives. This speaks to processes, people, capabilities, and culture. The chasm of change required is simply too wide to cross without more capital and more assistance, and companies get stuck between their successes in the present and the changes that are needed to achieve their full potential in the future. They lose their way and either stagnate or start losing market share to other nimbler competitors. Change is hard at any level of a company, and it creates business and professional risk. As a result, no change is made. It takes a catalyst to initiate the needed changes and a framework to effectively operationalize those changes.

At an inflection point, the current leaders—and, for that matter, almost everyone in the company—often need skills they don't have, because this is a revolutionary system that requires everyone to commit to new ways of thinking and acting. QHP works with clients throughout the transformation process because we understand that companies don't initially have the ability to establish and maintain this revolutionary new management system without advice and support— although it's essential for long-term success that they make the system fully their own.

The Competitive Advantage of Partnering

The leaders of successful companies at an inflection point realize that they need an infusion of capital to fuel their growth, but they're also smart enough to know that "business as usual" is not going to transform the company, even *with* an infusion of capital. This is the kind of company leader that QHP chooses to work with, because they are ready for dramatic growth. We align with the company on strategy, partner with management, and take execution risk. The execution risk associated with enabling a company to cross the chasm between where they are today and where they need to be to realize their full potential is significant.

This is why we strongly recommend The Management System, because this system can make it happen. We know it works. (I always tell the CEOs we work with at the outset that if they think they have a better management system to work with, they should use it—but not one of them has ever thought they did.) Private equity investors expect outsized returns in just three to five years. For such investors, every moment counts. Partnering with such an investor—one that offers expertise as well as capital—makes it much more likely that a company will reap the benefits of the investment capital and achieve rapid growth.

Using The Management System enables QHP to have a real partnership with the companies we invest in. We build the system together, tailoring it to their specific industry and needs. We build it together and then they operate it on their own, but they are always backed by the wisdom and expertise we offer about how The Management System works most effectively and what kind of specific results it should produce for the company.

My fellow QHP Partner Michael Sorensen has worked at other investment firms, and he succinctly sums up how QHP's approach differs from the standard approach:

> We've got a proven system, and we're going to help you make it *your* system. We're going to facilitate that transition. We're going to provide you with all the resources and expertise you need to accomplish this—anything you identify that you need to turn your business into a great business. Other funds don't do this. They say, "Okay, we have a hundred-day plan." And they come in and they do consulting work. They come in from the outside and identify something—a pricing initiative, for example, or something else—and they try to force it into your business. And then they go away. But with QHP, we go in, we get to know your business, we lay the foundation, we help you learn how to identify initiatives, how to recognize problems and solve them, how to take advantage of your strengths and minimize your weaknesses. And then it becomes this snowball effect of big and little things that continually improve the company. It's a unique and highly effective approach.

These are the kinds of questions you must be able to answer if you want to grow rapidly, and QHP helps you find the answers:

- How do you marshal your limited resources against limitless opportunity?

- How do you rapidly get your leaders on the same page of execution priorities and keep them focused—relentlessly focused?

- How do you rapidly make adjustments to your operational plan and align all your resources accordingly?

- How do you maximize the full potential of your capabilities?

In the book *The Advantage*, Patrick Lencioni writes about the most important step to high performance for a company: "create complete strategic clarity across the organization." He contends that this clarity can be created in an organization by answering these six questions:

- Why do we exist?

- How do we behave?

- What do we do?

- How will we succeed?

- What is most important, right now?

- Who must do what?

Answering these questions is an important component of the management off-site, where QHP's partner companies assess where they are and where they're going. We'll detail this off-site later in the book.

When I was working to create a system to effectively manage the business I was running as a first-time CEO, I did not have the benefit of Mr. Lencioni's book. However, judging from my own experience, he is on point. These are the questions that must be answered. But the challenge that remains is: How do you execute against them? The Management System provides an approach and concrete tools that enable you to achieve all these things—and more.

As I mentioned before, QHP's experience working with founder-owned and family-owned companies have shown that the decision-making has been aggregated into a small number of individuals. There's a reluctance to trust others, engage others, and enable others to take on more responsibility for capitalizing on growth opportunities. When we engage with a company, they know that they have an opportunity to grow and the capital to make it happen. But money alone is not going to get it done, which is why having a partner that brings both equity *and* capability to the table is so advantageous. Rather than a hit-and-run approach to investing, we stick with companies for the long run, meeting with them regularly to make sure The Management System is being effectively deployed and reviewing the metrics the system produces to make sure they stay on track for rapid growth.

An example of this is how we brought a new CEO into a pharmaceutical company that had ostensibly adopted The Management System, but also had a founder who could not develop the habit of using the system's tools to continually improve the company. This is how that new CEO describes his experience:

> The former CEO, who was also the founder of the company, was in place for about ten months before I was brought in. The Management System didn't change under me, but the impact and the way it actually influenced the company and the decision-making process changed dramatically. The role of the CEO when working with The Management System is about mindset, about using it to find ways to affect improvement in the company. But under the prior CEO's leadership,

there was no discussion between management reviews about what was happening, no attempt to use the information from Management System tools such as Tracking Sheets and A3s to move the company forward.

I was very clear with our executive team that this was not going to be the way we operated the company anymore. We were going to take advantage of the common language that The Management System provided to talk about a forecast, about not making goals, about shortfalls in the business. We were going to use the system tools to help us all understand where we were and what we needed to do to improve.

In addition to capital needed to invest in equipment, people, processes, or geographic expansion—or all these things—companies at an inflection point need guidance about how to get *from* here *to* there. And in a lot of cases, they need additional talent to be able to do that. They're constrained by their own experience and bias there, by the very ways of doing things that have enabled them to achieve the level of success they're currently enjoying. They are often frustrated by their inability to take advantage of opportunities that they know they should be able to take advantage of. They have to shift the way they operate to rapidly scale the enterprise. The ability to rapidly scale is the key to success, and it is also the thing that such companies are least likely to be able to achieve on their own.

Rapid scaling is what The Management System makes possible. As I've said, it's not an evolutionary approach but a revolutionary one. And only revolutionary changes in the way a company operates will make rapid scaling and growth possible. CEOs who believe that their company has the potential to capture a huge new market, or make a highly profitable strategy shift, recognize that they need a partner to help them get there, a partner that's going to bring more than just money. And that's what makes QHP a different kind of private equity firm. It's not just about money for us. It's about combining money with talent and effective processes that will enable a company to *capitalize* on that money by seizing the opportunities available.

My QHP colleague Jeff Edwards learned about the difference between the QHP approach and what he calls the "Wall Street" attitude when he was new to the firm, and I asked him to define EBITDA:

> I grew up predominantly in the financial industry. When I got to QHP and Vern showed me The Management System for the first time, he asked me, "How do you define EBITDA?" And I said, "Vern, we can do this in fifteen minutes." Like it was easy. Like all it involved was putting down financial metrics on a piece of paper. And I used to think it was just financial metrics, but it's not. EBITDA is defined by things like HR hiring the right people for the divisions they hire for, about whether effective training is happening in all the divisions, about whether finance is getting the audit done on time or not. EBITDA is defined by how the business operates, not by financial metrics.
>
> And that's what I missed when I said we could do this in fifteen minutes. It's just so powerful what The Management System approach does for private equity and investors. I think we understand the businesses that we go into so well. We truly partner with them. We don't just deal with them by exception, on one issue here or there; we're all in. And companies that embrace the system are outperforming any of their peers, even in down markets.

The founders and/or owners of a company often don't fully understand the operational dynamics of their business. Up to the inflection point, they've run the business effectively using a lot of intuitive expertise and good judgment. But they often don't understand the operational processes that will enable their company to scale and grow. And that's what The Management System enables them to do, to unleash operational and performance leverage for growth.

The Tools for Ensuring Growth

Companies have limitless potential but always limited resources. And things never go completely to plan, so you need a system that recognizes when things are going wrong and makes it possible to adjust quickly. It may sound simple to expand a business that is already successful, but some things always go wrong here and there when scaling an enterprise. So you need a framework that tells you exactly when and where things are not going according to plan, which enables you to correct your course.

You need to make data-driven decisions in a nanosecond and immediately align execution across the entire organization. In growth-oriented companies, long decision timeframes are your enemy. As in most process-improvement efforts, you want as few steps and layers as possible. The same is true for decision-making. We work in an era of instantaneous information availability. To execute successfully against a compelling market opportunity, your organization needs the information required to stay focused on the most important work activities and stay aligned with your growth/transformation objectives.

Decisions also need to be made quickly and made deeper into the organization and closer to customers—where the action is. Middle managers need to be empowered yet still held accountable. They need to know how to work together effectively with their teams, how they are held accountable within their teams and by other teams, how they are dependent on other teams, and how other teams are dependent on them. Reports of no consequence, meetings with no purpose, and responsibilities without accountability will *not* produce excellence within an organization. The Management System is designed to help you clarify your direction and strategy, create brief, focused reports that capture the key growth factors, limit meetings to the essential, and ensure that all roles and responsibilities are clear and accountable.

The implementation of The Management System uses a number of key documents to ensure that a company gets on the right track at the outset of its transformation process and stays on track over time to achieve the success it has envisioned for itself—what we call the company's "True North" goals. The key documents at the outset of the process are:

- **From-To Chart**: Delineates where the company currently is and where it wants to end up in three to seven years. It is an overview of what your company and its investors plan to achieve.

- **Vision/Mission/Purpose Statement**: Serves to unite every member of your company around the work to be done to capitalize on the full potential of the company and its overall goals. Lays out how your company defines itself and what it wants to achieve.

- **Values/Behavior Statement**: Defines at a high level the "personality" and culture of your company. Establishes how the company is going to do its work going forward and how your people are going to act with one another, partners, and customers—the standards they're going to hold themselves to as they operate.

- **SWOT Analysis**: You're probably familiar with this document, in which you analyze your company's strengths, weaknesses, opportunities for success, and threats to achieving that success. It provides a starting point for your transformation/growth.

The documents that are key to operationalizing The Management System are:

- **True North**: Fully lays out your financial, operational, customer, and employee goals. It is the document against which you measure your company's performance throughout the transformation process.

- **Functional Construct**: Charts the way your company is organized and how it functions—the departments, workflows, and interdependencies that enable you to execute your plan.

- **Roles and Responsibilities Sheet**: Makes crystal clear who is in charge of what functions within your company and what they are expected to accomplish. It includes responsibilities, dependencies, accountabilities, major decision rights, and the skills required to assume each role and discharge its responsibilities.

- **Tracking Sheet**: Shows financial, operational, customer engagement, and employee engagement goals for each functional area, with the top ten metrics for that function. Each metric is expressed monthly across the year and color coded to enable rapid understanding of performance against plan, highlighting both issues and opportunities.

- **Alignment Sheet**: Relates each performance metric to the goals laid out in your True North document.

- **A3s**: There are three types of A3s: Remediation, Project, and Strategy. Each is built on a single piece of paper that defines the metric, the gap against the plan metric, the background of the situation, the root cause of the metric not being achieved, and a plan to bridge the gap.

In the following chapter, I will explain each of these tools in more detail, and in subsequent chapters I will teach you how to use them effectively during your transformation process. I've also included examples of these documents throughout the book and in the Appendix section.

As the examples I provided at the beginning of this chapter demonstrate, dramatic transformation and growth is entirely possible for a successful company. But achieving it requires a dramatic change in mindset, a strong commitment, and a blueprint for change that is geared toward rapid scaling and accountability. The Management System provides that blueprint, and *Accelerating Growth* will show you how it works.

2

THE TOOLS FOR TRANSFORMATION

When you renovate a building—in effect, transforming it—you need tools that work well and make that renovation easier and faster. Transforming an organization also requires effective tools. I named the tools used in The Management System at the end of chapter 1, and in this chapter, I will describe each tool briefly. Ensuing chapters will go into detail about individual tools.

The first set of tools are analytical ones that prepare you for the actual work of transforming your company using The Management System. They help your management team clarify where the company is in the market, where it wants to be in the market (including what new kinds of markets it might create for itself), and how the company will comport itself as it works toward its goals.

These analytical tools are:

- From-To Chart

- Vision/Mission/Purpose Statement

- Values/Behavior Statement

- SWOT Analysis

From-To Chart

When QHP decides to invest in and work with a company, we need to be clear about where we want to take the company over the term of our investment of time and money. QHP does due diligence research on the market and the company, as well as what the company believes about itself and its potential. The combination of those perspectives forms the basis of where we think we can help take the company, how much we think it can grow in the near future.

The From-To Chart forms the basis of a fundamental understanding between us and our portfolio company about where the company has the opportunity to go. It summarizes the tremendous possibilities for success and is a great motivator for getting the company to realize its full potential. The chart also enables us to frame our perspective on growth—the contrast between where the company is and where it's going. If done thoughtfully, the From-To Chart reveals the gaps that need to be bridged by revolutionary change to capitalize on the company's market potential. This is an important document for winning the executive team's commitment to both the company's potential and its need to change in order to reach that potential.

Here is an example of a From-To Chart:

Combining findings from our diligence effort with our proposed strategy have helped us define our future state

		Today	Future State (2027)
1	**Market opportunity**	• CVS, CNS, GI, and Institutional TAs • Emerging scale and diversification • Rising rank on industry radar	• Dosage and TA "agnostic" (for adjacent TAs) • Established scale and diversification • Leadership (top 10) position in "white space"
2	**Offering**	• 10 FDA-approved products • <10 late/midstage pipeline assets	• ~30 FDA-approved products • ~30 pipeline assets
3	**Business model**	• Opportunistic and sequential evolution from acquisitions	• Deliberate and intentional approach driven by clear strategic aspiration
4	**Enablers (capabilities, processes, systems)**	• Initial signs of SG&A-lite model • Initial cadence of R&D and BD output • Views on "optimally integrated" model	• Leading commercial capability driven by omni-channel, ecosystem, and digital/data • Proven R&D and BD w/ scale and predictability • Proven "optimally integrated" model
5	**Financials**	• $409M Revenue • <40% Adj. EBITDA margin • Emerging diversification	• ~$1,000M Revenue • 40% + Adj. EBITDA margin • High diversification

Vision/Mission/Purpose Statement

An effective Vision/Mission/Purpose Statement is your company's strategic compass. It's important for your functional management team to come together and lock it down with one another, because this consolidates the management team, aligns them, and motivates them to act.

It is essential to define and agree upon these elements from the very beginning of the process. Often, for the type and size of companies we work with, little real thought has been given to these elements and very little, if any, action or effort has been made to direct the company according to them. But companies that are poised for transformation and/or rapid growth *must* take the time to clearly define these elements and seek agreement on them.

An effective Vision/Mission/Purpose Statement must have input from and be reflective of the whole team. It unites every member of that team around the work that must be done to realize the company's full potential. In some cases, this may be the first time that a broader set of management has come together to discuss, debate, agree upon, and align with *any* corporate decision. This statement is the glue that binds everyone together and motivates real-time production from the whole work force.

Here is an example of a Vision/Mission/Purpose Statement:

InformedDNA Mission and Vision

InformedDNA is revolutionizing the application of genomic insights to enhance patient care and improve outcomes for all, shaping the future of precision healthcare.

Mission
We are revolutionizing the application of genomic insights to enhance patient care and improve outcomes for all.

Vision
To shape the future of precision healthcare.

Values/Behavior Statement

Values define how you're going to do your work, how you're going to act with one another, and the standards that you'll hold yourselves accountable to as you deal with your partners and customers. Discussions around values and behaviors are a significant defining point for a management team in a company that is at the inflection point of growth or transformation. Defining your values and articulating the expected behaviors for each stakeholder builds a fundamental basis for the company culture as your organization transforms itself and grows rapidly. Later in the book, I will discuss the challenges associated with holding people to these performance expectations and the effect it will have on your transformation effort if you do not.

Here is an example of a Values/Behavior Statement:

"Lexitas"

Ophthalmic Focused
Infuse opthalmic expertise in every facet of our business
- Serve as a thought leader
- Build, buy, and partner to expand our ophthalmic offerings
- Develop our brand to share and showcase ophthalmic expertise

People Focused
Partner with those who value our culture
- Listen and demonstrate a willingness to learn
- Build strong relationships with ophthalmic stakeholders
- Solve problems together

Purpose Driven
Possess a sense of urgency and intentionality in all interactions
- Understand and pursue customer objectives
- Deliver results through innovative strategies
- Grow ophthalmic expertise throughout our company

SWOT Analysis

When your people are aligned around where they want to go, they need a really honest analysis of where they *are*, what their starting place is, and what kind of challenges they face to get to where they're going. The SWOT Analysis is a well-known tool for nailing down your company's current strengths and weaknesses (SW) as well as its near-term opportunities and threats (OT). QHP recommends that you establish the top five in each of these categories at the outset—but the SWOT Analysis should live on and change as your company changes and grows. This is where you gear up for implementing The Management System, where you create very specific goals based on the opportunities and threats you've identified, where you examine your strengths and weaknesses in order to take advantage of the former and overcome the latter. This keeps your company grounded in the reality of where it is now and where it is going.

Here is an example of a SWOT Analysis:

SWOT

Strengths	Weaknesses
• Leading concentration of genomic expertise • Impactful relationships with providers/patients • Massive collection of real-world genetic data • Trusted and recognized brand • Shovel ready for change/innovation	• Product development and commercialization (lack of go-to-market strategy and product packaging) • Out-of-date tech stack (not integrated, redundancy, etc) • Organizational Instability (lack of coordination and unclear ownership) • Consolidated revenue streams (lack of customer diversification) • Clinical and business talent gaps (much of our staff repurposed into roles not in their background)
Opportunities	Threats
• Leverage current market leadership position to drive demand for precision healthcare ("Lead Dog") regional payors, larger employers • Utilize digital capabilities to expand the number of patients at the top of the funnel • Monetize our current proprietary data assets and grow them further to impact financial/clinical outcomes • End-to-end strategic precision medicine partner for health plan—not a point solution • Align IDNA capabilities with how payers buy and use	• Insourcing • Regulatory/legislative changes • Coverage mandate/accelerated adoption • Privacy concerns on behalf of the general public • Health plan risk tolerance with data sharing

The second set of tools we use are those that power The Management System and make it possible for your company to transform/grow at a rate far faster than it was capable of before. These tools are:

- True North

- Functional Construct

- Roles and Responsibilities Sheet

- Tracking Sheet

- A3s

- Alignment Sheet

I will describe each of these tools and their functions here.

TRUE NORTH

I have always been goal-oriented myself, and I've found throughout my career that for competitive individuals and companies, establishing clear goals is the first step toward success. As the old adage goes, if you don't know where you're going, any road will take you there—and that's a road that leads nowhere. We often find that the companies we invest in have never had a clear articulation of their goals, a clear definition of what they believe constitutes successful performance. As is natural, the primary focus of these companies before hitting their growth inflection point has been on the generation of cash and the ability to make payroll. But in order to transform itself, a company needs to establish a clear picture of what it wants to achieve financially. We call this picture the True North.

For our purposes at QHP, the definition of True North is easy. Companies that want to work with us are "selling" us what I like to call a "hockey stick" of growth (because of its shape on a graph, which shows steep growth), both in the form of revenue and profitability—meaning the ability to increase revenue and profitability quickly and dramatically with the right investment and the right guidance. QHP invests in partners whose management teams believe they can achieve this hockey stick of growth. Therefore, the revenue and the EBITDA that they believe they can achieve become our True North objectives on the chart.

Some companies include other True North objectives on the chart, such as employee and customer engagement and satisfaction and bookings. But revenue and EBITDA are always the starting points because every company tracks them and has goals for them. Companies don't often have a foundation for measuring things like employee and customer satisfaction, so they need to establish a baseline for those measures in order to start collecting meaningful data on them. That takes time, and you can add the other measures later.

Here is an example of a True North:

($ millions)	2023	2024	2025	2026	2027
Net Revenue	$409.0	$462.0	$572.0	$849.0	$1066.0
Adjusted EBITDA	$145.0	$175.0	$226.0	$370.0	$484.0

FUNCTIONAL CONSTRUCT

Establishing the Functional Construct defines how the work is done within a company. The Functional Construct comprises three major functional categories of work:

- **Enablement functions**: These functions define what products and services are effectively enabling the company to do business. Examples of enabling functions are strategy, product management, development, and marketing.

- **Execution functions**: These are the functions that execute the business of your company and are the ones that actually touch customers. Examples of these functions are sales, delivery, implementation, and customer support.

- **Supporting functions**: Every company requires functions that support enabling and executing work. Examples of such functions are finance, legal, IT, facilities, human resources, quality management, and regulatory compliance.

Within companies that are at a growth inflection point, the work and primary decision-making is usually relegated to a few critically important individuals, so the company is fundamentally people-dependent. One very important growth premise is that you cannot scale a company if it is dependent on specific individuals. You can only do it when the company becomes process-dependent and you put your best talent, whoever that might be, into the processes where they can make the greatest contribution to the company's transformation/growth.

With the Functional Construct, you define how the work happens in your company. There is a point at which your work starts, and there's also a point where your work ends. Enablement functions start the work of your company and are followed by the execution functions. The work of the company starts with strategy and ends with a delighted customer as a result of your enablement and execution work efforts.

All the enablement and execution functions are assisted by the supporting functions. While the relationship between the enablement and execution functions is linear, their relationships with the supporting functions are episodic, meaning that sometimes they need a supporting function a lot and sometimes they don't need it at all. Supporting functions (such as HR) also support the whole company in various ways on an ongoing basis.

Here is an example of a simple Functional Construct:

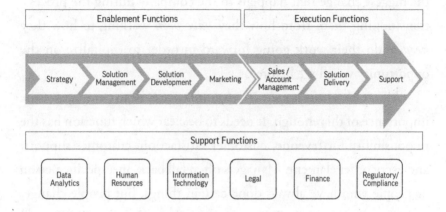

ROLES AND RESPONSIBILITIES SHEET

Once you have agreed on how the work of your company is to be done and have clear definitions of the enablement, execution, and supporting functions, you must define the specific work that is to be accomplished within each function. A Roles and Responsibilities Sheet is made up of the following components:

- Role definition

- Responsibilities

- Dependencies

- Accountabilities

- Decision rights

- Skill requirements

Defining these roles and responsibilities is a difficult thing to do—and it is also one of the most important things you will do—because it requires very clear accountability that can be monitored. This is where we spend the most time working with our companies when implementing The Management System, because it comprises the biggest change that happens to the company during the process: transitioning them from how they *have been* working to how they *need to* do their work going forward in order to capitalize on the opportunity we all see before us.

It's not about the people; it's about the work! I can't emphasize the importance of this enough. It needs to be clear which function has the responsibility for revenue, customer satisfaction, customer support, and every other element. Managers often fall back on a specific person or people who have always done certain things, but people change, and a function does not. Being clear on roles and responsibilities will establish exactly what kind of talent you need to successfully get the work done and meet the goals of each function.

Here is an example of a Roles and Responsibilities Sheet:

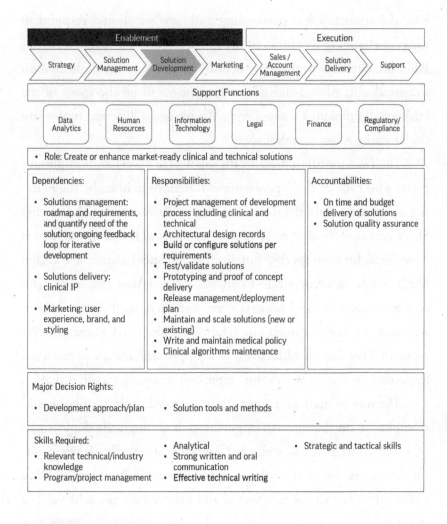

Enablement					Execution	
Strategy	Solution Management	Solution Development	Marketing	Sales / Account Management	Solution Delivery	Support

Support Functions

Data Analytics	Human Resources	Information Technology	Legal	Finance	Regulatory/ Compliance

- Role: Create or enhance market-ready clinical and technical solutions

Dependencies:	Responsibilities:	Accountabilities:
• Solutions management: roadmap and requirements, and quantify need of the solution; ongoing feedback loop for iterative development • Solutions delivery: clinical IP • Marketing: user experience, brand, and styling	• Project management of development process including clinical and technical • Architectural design records • Build or configure solutions per requirements • Test/validate solutions • Prototyping and proof of concept delivery • Release management/deployment plan • Maintain and scale solutions (new or existing) • Write and maintain medical policy • Clinical algorithms maintenance	• On time and budget delivery of solutions • Solution quality assurance

Major Decision Rights:

- Development approach/plan   • Solution tools and methods

Skills Required:

- Relevant technical/industry knowledge
- Program/project management

• Analytical
• Strong written and oral communication
• Effective technical writing

• Strategic and tactical skills

TRACKING SHEET

When I first envisioned The Management System, the concept of a Tracking Sheet was foremost in my mind. I wanted to know—and I wanted everyone in the organization to know—if we were performing successfully against our objectives or not, and I wanted to be able to see that instantly. In the competitive environment that I was in, it was quite clear to me that it would not be efficient or effective to review twelve three-ring binders full of spreadsheets and charts to determine how the company was performing and how we should respond to the ever-changing dynamics of the marketplace. Nor would a Power-Point presentation do the trick, because it's still too much information to spread out. Also, I did not want *opinions* to be the focus of the business discussion; I wanted *facts*. We needed a different tool—and the Tracking Sheet was that tool.

The Tracking Sheet presents the top ten (or fewer) most important metrics for each of the organizational functions defined by the Functional Construct and the Roles and Responsibilities Sheet. A Tracking Sheet contains *the most important metrics critical for the attainment of True North* for each specific function. For proper balance, a Tracking Sheet needs to incorporate financial, operational, employee, and customer metrics. And because every executive in the organization who is on a variable compensation bonus is paid based on the achievement of True North objectives, it is important for *all* operational leadership to agree on the most important metrics for each function.

The way to manage a company at a growth inflection point and to capitalize on that growth opportunity is through the deployment of a well-conceived and well-used Tracking Sheet. This is where the rubber meets the road, and you measure exactly how you're doing against the plan you've established and believe you can achieve. The metrics *must* be objective, *not* subjective. They must be numbers, not just opinions. The benefit of using a Tracking Sheet is that you can see the metrics for every function in the organization within a one-hour meeting, learning everything important about how the company is performing at the moment. This is pure gold for a management team trying to grow a company!

Here is an example of a Tracking Sheet:

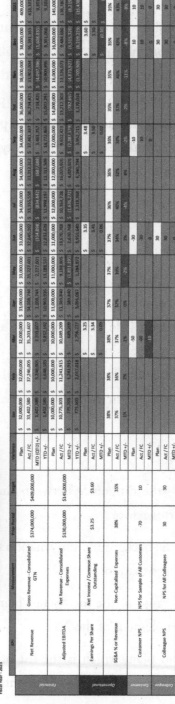

A3s

I mentioned the business writing of Pascal Dennis earlier, and I learned the A3 concept from him as I read his book. The idea is that the means of dealing with any problematic situation should be summed up clearly and succinctly on a single piece of paper, therefore named for the designated size of standard European paper, which is A3. The Management System utilizes three different types of A3s:

- Remediation (or Red)

- Project

- Strategy

Remediation (or Red) A3

This is the most commonly used A3, which I always refer to as the "Red" A3. The reason I do this is because, as I described above, if a Tracking Sheet metric is not on plan, it is coded red. If a top ten metric on your Tracking Sheet is red, then the functional executive responsible for that metric must produce an A3. An A3 has the following elements on it:

- The metric

- The gap—the difference between the plan metric and the actual performance

- Any specific background information that will help articulate the current situation

- The root cause of the metric not being achieved—*the* most important element of the A3

- The action plan, which is the list of activities that will be performed to get the metric back onto plan

- Any resources required to achieve this that are not under the control of the functional leader presenting the A3

Having just a single piece of paper with all these elements on it enables you to establish a common vocabulary for problem-solving across the organization. You can sit down with any group in the organization and show them the metric, the background of the situation, the action plan, and who needs to contribute to the action plan, and then manage progress against the action plan. No more PowerPoint presentations expressing the personal opinions or biases of a leader. No more overly detailed Excel spreadsheets with pivot tables to navigate through. One piece of paper with all the elements required to understand the situation and determine whether the right plan is being put in place to remediate a specific operational metric.

On the next page, you'll find an example of a Remedial A3:

Action A3
Aged AR
June 2022

Performance/Gaps/Targets

Problem Statement

91% of A/R balance was within target timeframe of < 60 days which signals that clients are not paying within agreed upon terms.

Goal

Goal is to have all accounts receivable current. We will consider this a success if 95% or more of the total accounts receivable balance is < 60 days aged.

Background

Rapid invoicing turnaround and payment by clients is key to support healthy cash flow. While collections have generally been very timely, we occasionally have payments from clients that are delayed for various reasons. For this month there are several clients with balances greater than 60 days aged – see those with balances over $50k.

Marken ($43k) has not responded to our requests; that relationship is with BD rep who has left Catalyst.

Client	Open value over 60 days
Client A	$332,461
Client B	$248,328
Client C	$174,056
Client D	$156,830
Client E	$155,912
Client F	$128,091
Client G	$119,061
Client H	$117,589
Client I	$99,631
Client J	$90,209
Client K	$51,788
Client L	$51,460
Client M	$50,000

Root Cause Analysis: Why? Why? Why?

- **Client is waiting for executed amendments before paying invoices**
  - Amendments are delayed due to P&C resource and lack of prioritization previously

- **Project finance has been slow to follow up on open invoices**
  - Insufficient time to follow up
  - Team turnover and new team members are still getting up to speed on processes, including collections

- **Client has complicated system which results in invoices being held up**
  - We have not built relationships with client to work together to solve this issue

Recommendations

- **Promote/Encourage Timely invoice review by Clients.** Continue to have ongoing discussions with Client's regarding status of invoices and potential queries related to invoice line items and related CCR delivery of those items wither ad hoc discussions with the Client or as an agenda item on routine Client/CCR project status meetings.
- **Re-communicate escalation plan for Aged AR to all teams**
- **Train Project Finance analysts on best practices for collections**
- **Project Finance to increase time commitment for collection efforts**
- **Get open amendments signed.** Project Finance and Proposals have started a weekly call to prioritize amendments with work at risk situations:

Action Plan

Action	Owner	Due Date	Status
PF to allocate 2 hours/week to collections to include a mid-month check in	PF	Ongoing	Decided, Started in July
Re-distribute process/escalation path for aged balances	PF	August 31st	Not yet started, focus on revenue/margin
Client A - set up regular meeting to review open invoices and discuss roadblocks for payment	PF/BD	August 31st	Not yet started
Client B – re-request to be paid via ACH	PF	August 15th	Not yet started
Client C – send legal letter	PF/Res Ops/Legal	7/15/2022	Letter sent, response date 8/9

Results

All AR < 60 days aged to ensure cash flow available for company operations

Project A3

A Project A3 has the same elements as the Remedial A3, but it is targeted toward executing an initiative that is typically cross-functional, where two or more functions within the company are working together on a project. For example, you might be trying to figure out how to line up organizational resources to install and use a new CRM, ERP, or payroll system, the kind of project that has an objective but involves people from many different parts of the company. The Project A3 shows the objective, the background relative to the importance of the objective, an articulation of how success will be defined, and the specific plan that needs to be executed to achieve that success.

Strategy A3

A Strategy A3 is similar to the Project A3, but it is focused on evaluating a larger strategic initiative. It typically incorporates a perspective that goes beyond the current operational or fiscal year, looking at something larger and more long term—an acquisition, for example. What's the strategy associated with acquiring this company? What are the benefits of acquiring it? What is the action plan required to achieve the acquisition? The A3 enables you to sum up on one sheet of paper the background of the acquisition proposal, a definition of the strategy involved in making the acquisition, a picture of what would be needed to implement the acquisition, and what a successful implementation would look like.

ALIGNMENT SHEET

In practice, Alignment Sheets are one of the more complicated tools to use, so it is often companies that are more mature in their use of The Management System processes who deploy them. But I encourage everyone to use them eventually, if not immediately, because they are very helpful when you are trying to drive decision-making responsibility down into the organization. Alignment Sheets show how each role is important in achieving True North due to the dependencies among different functions within the organization. Alignment Sheets provide a vertical view of how the company operates.

Alignment Sheets are a great tool to ensure that each function in your organization has a set of balanced metrics that are aligned to True North. They are very helpful as you cascade Tracking Sheets deeper into your organization. They are especially powerful as you deploy The Management System throughout your organization and seek to align the work of junior managers and individual contributors with the work of senior managers and your ultimate objective: achievement of your True North goals. In my view, the ideal organization is one in which every member of the company has an individual Alignment Sheet to work with, because that means they know what's important to be working on—and consequently (and equally significant) what is *not* important. With the information on an Alignment Sheet, they will understand how critical their own set of responsibilities is, how important it is that they perform successfully against their objectives and thereby align themselves with the company's goals.

When I say that The Management System eliminates politics and parochialism, it is the deployment of the Tracking Sheets and the alignment of objectives at all levels in the organization that clearly articulate the importance of every team member's contribution. Nothing is more powerful than having every person in the organization know what their job is and what their job isn't, and how their work relates to the functional objectives of the organization and to the overall success of the company.

Here is an example of an Alignment Sheet:

Priorities for CEO

Priorities for CEO	TARGET	TEAMS (1–15)
1	Net Revenues	$129,000	
2	Adjusted EBITDA	$51,500	
3	Free Cash Flows	$17,500	
4	Employee NPS (Corporate)	30.0%	
5	Litigation Expenses	$5,100	
6			
7			
8			
9			
10			

TRUE NORTH

TRUE NORTH	TARGET	TEAMS (A–H)
Revenue	$129,000	
Adjusted EBITDA	$51,500	
Free Cash Flows	$22,150	
Employee NPS	30.0%	
Covenant EBITDA	$45,300	

Priorities for CFO

	Priorities for CFO	TARGET	A	B	C	D	E	F	G	H
1	Prompt Pay / Product Returns Discount	5.50%	X							
2	OPEX - CFO	$7,444	X							
3	Days Liquidity On-hand - Cash and Cash Equivalents	78			X	X				
4	Days Outstanding - AR net of Cash Expenses Accrued	TBD			X	X				
5	AEBITDA - Forecast Accuracy	TBD			X					
6	Management System Adherence	TBD						X		
7	CAPEX - Consolidated	$9,000		X						
8	NQ Discretionary	$1,500						X		
9	Acquisition Expenses	$750								
10										

Category (1–10)									
Operations/Process		X	X	X	X	X			
People									
Customers & Mkts									
Financials	X	X						X	X

Putting the Tools to Use

The functional leadership of a company in the process of transforming itself comes together once a month to have what I call an operating committee meeting to review the Tracking Sheets for each of the functions and analyze how they're performing against the True North objectives. This meeting happens in the third or fourth week of every month and reviews the previous month. So, for example, at a February 21 meeting, you'd be looking at January's final numbers, forecasting for February, and making necessary adjustments to the business based on performance.

Each functional leader prepares for this meeting by gathering and evaluating the top ten metrics on their Tracking Sheets, preparing their Remediation A3s for anything that's not going according to plan, and being prepared to present to the leadership team. This way, there's a rhythm to the business that is efficient and effective and liberating—not a whole bunch of meetings and long reports, but relatively brief meetings in which you talk about taking action, where all the functional leaders are able to see the totality of the business transparently. From each meeting, everyone makes adjustments to their operating priorities going forward, and goes back to work based upon those realignments.

This rhythm of doing business is liberating for management teams because it involves a very efficient and effective set of discussions to help them move forward. There is just this one meeting a month where everybody sees how the business is operating end to end. It enables them to make necessary adjustments, capitalize on opportunities, mitigate threats, and find resources. This meeting is where the dials are read and the knobs turned to adjust the way the "machinery" of the business is running.

There are five rules to live by when you put The Management System into action:

1. **The only thing that cannot change is True North.**

   At QHP, our investment decisions are predicated on the projections that we come up with in partnership with a company. Post-investment, our job is to work with the company's management team to deliver on those projections, such as the projected revenue and EBITDA growth that comprise the company's True North. When we work with the company to implement The Management System, any aspect of the system can be changed except for True North. There is no debate or discussion about this once it has been established. True North is locked for the duration of the investment. This becomes the "Holy Grail," the objectives to which the entire company has made a commitment and toward which The Management System and all the company's activities are directed.

2. **If a task is important enough to be a responsibility, accountability, or dependency, it can only land on one function.**

   I mentioned this earlier, but it's important enough to bear repeating. When you develop your Roles and Responsibilities Sheets, you are implementing a change from how your company has operated in the past and laying out how it will transform/grow itself going forward. In most companies we deal with, a few executives within the company have been making all the decisions that have enabled the success achieved thus far. But that approach cannot be scaled. As you develop your new roles and responsibilities and specifically

43

define the work that has to be accomplished within each function, it is essential that you remember one thing: if there's an important task to be performed, it *must* be owned by a single function, not spread out over two or more functions. Important tasks *must* be clearly owned by the functional executives accountable for delivering on those tasks.

In virtually every situation I have encountered, when responsibilities are shared among multiple functions or executives, *no one* owns the work; *no one* feels truly responsible and accountable for that work getting done—and getting done right. Therefore, unnecessary dysfunction and inefficiencies are injected into the organization. One of the major advantages of The Management System is that it eliminates ways of operating that drive dysfunction. This system requires that if there's an important task that needs to be done, you *must* be clear about which *single* function is responsible for completing that work. This is one of the challenging parts of implementing The Management System: a lot of people's "cheese" gets moved, and they must adjust to the changes in their roles and responsibilities.

3. **There is no truth without debate.**

I attribute this aphorism, which I love, to Antonio Perez, who was the CEO of Kodak during my tenure there. It makes the very important point that everyone's perspective must be valued during the transformation/growth process, because everyone's commitment is necessary to achieve the level of engagement and alignment required for transformation and growth. You want to encourage everyone to speak up, to say what's on their mind, to challenge ideas and perspectives, because this is in the best interest of the company.

I've already mentioned how critical an effective middle management team is to success in this venture, and I'll discuss that more later. To have a functional and successful middle management team, to allow the kind of effective business discussion and debate that leads to success, everyone must feel comfortable speaking up and having their perspective valued. "There is no truth without debate" means that there cannot be true alignment and full commitment without the inclusion and consideration of all perspectives.

4. **Great companies work frictionlessly across functions.**
Most companies are organized in a hierarchy, and decisions are typically made by those at the top of the organization. This means that there's a lot of discussion that has to go way up the organizational structure and then back down that structure in order for decisions to be made and actions to be taken. In The Management System, the work is organized linearly through the enablement of execution functions. You want decisions made as close to the customer as possible, and you want each function to understand how it relates to the other functions—especially those that are on either side of any given function. Good companies are those that are good at their functional performance, but great companies are the ones that work frictionlessly across the functions. This means that decisions are made deep within the organization and close to where the work is being done and where the customers are—not at the top of a hierarchy, where those making the decisions are furthest away from where the work is being done and where the customers are.

5. **Be process-dependent, not people-dependent.**

I mentioned previously that most companies with the profile that QHP invests in are very dependent on their owners, founders, or CEO and maybe a few other top executives for all their decisions. A handful of close associates and executives have made virtually every decision inside the organization. Therefore, these companies are totally dependent on those people. If they lose one of the members of that small group, there is no one capable of taking up the reins! You simply cannot scale or transform or grow an organization when it is totally dependent on a small group of people. You can only do it when the organization is dependent on well-thought-out and established processes and has the best people performing the work of each function within those processes.

It is also important that all functions are connected and aligned, because you cannot scale an organization in which, for example, you're effective within the execution functions but not within the enablement functions, or vice versa. All functions must be effective and interconnected. When the functions are well connected, performing their specific work, and making decisions across those functions, as opposed to moving up and down a hierarchy, it is amazing how quickly a company can scale.

Private equity investment returns are expected within a three- to seven-year horizon, the average being about five years, which is a relatively short period of time for a business to change. This means that investors cannot waste a minute in the process of helping a company reorganize and execute against the business's potential. The best way for investors to understand a business and partner with its management team is to jointly implement The Management System with that company. At QHP, our practice is to prepare for and set up The Management System initially during a one-week management off-site. We will take people fully away from their daily work of running the company and keep them separated from the rest of the company. (And somehow the company always manages to survive!)

We know that the week will start with building the From-To Chart, and we know that the week will end with the complete implementation of The Management System, but the journey between those two points is never the same. Most management teams have never taken that much time away from the daily business to organize themselves and plan their work. To make that week the most effective it can be, a framework is required. At QHP, that framework is The Management System. We take the functional leaders through the process of implementing all the elements of the system. They leave at the end of the week with a fully operationalized plan for how they are going to get their work done so that over the next twelve months, they can execute against the True North objectives they've established.

A significant side benefit of this week is that QHP, as a private equity investor and partner of the company, learns everything we need to know about how that company operates, its strengths and weaknesses, its team members and their working relationships, and where we need to focus our time and energies to create value for the company. When the management team leaves this off-site, every executive understands how the work of the company is now going to be done end to end—and this is often *the first time* they have fully understood this! As a result, from that point on, not a day is wasted with work and effort that is not prioritized toward the successful achievement of True North.

After the off-site, there is a clear plan for achieving the development and growth objectives—and the management team starts working this way the Monday after the off-site! The scaling of the business starts *immediately*. The plan for how to do this is not locked down for the year; it is only locked down for the moment. This is our collective best view of how to begin attacking the opportunity with the resources that the company has. And that "how" may be adjusted tomorrow or next week, or at the first operating committee meeting next month. But the thing that doesn't change is True North. That is where the company sets its compass, and that is the direction in which it goes.

3

CLARIFYING VISION AND STRATEGY

To some businesspeople, the Vision/Mission/Purpose and Values/Behavior Statements might seem superfluous. This especially can be true of companies that have been charging ahead so fast that they believe they can only focus on the day-to-day with no time to consider the bigger picture. But at QHP, we insist on it. After we've established—together—what the company's potential is and where we want it to end up by developing the From-To Chart, I meet with the CEO before the off-site meeting to make sure we're on the same page, that the CEO understands The Management System and is on board with implementing it.

The CEO won't push back on the From-To Chart because we developed it together, but the Vision/Mission/Purpose and Values/Behavior Statements, which are the first things we take up at the off-site, can be more problematic. The discussions at the off-site involve more management team members and more points of view than the CEO may be used to hearing. But it's extremely important for middle management to participate in the discussion of what the company is all about and, when we get to the Values/Behavior Statement, how it ought to operate. Having this discussion achieves buy-in from the middle management team—which is essential to success—because they get heard and leave the off-site in full agreement with what the company is all about and how it should operate. We don't move on to the next step until all this has been agreed upon, because it must be institutionalized (remember: process-oriented rather than people-oriented) in order to accomplish the work that must be done.

Here is an example of how one company's mission and values statement changed over the course of its off-site with us. This is how that statement read going into the off-site:

Inherited Mission and Vision Statements

Mission

InformedDNA optimizes clinical decisions through impactful solutions leveraging the most current genomics expertise. We are the nation's leading applied genomics company, with the largest independent team of genetics specialists representing the full breadth of specialties and subspecialties, and backed by more than fourteen years of clinical data and financial proof of effectiveness.

Vision

With the nation's largest and most experienced team of genetics specialists, and the right technologies to deliver real-time genomics insights and solutions, we're helping health plans, life sciences organizations, and healthcare providers to optimize clinical decisions and fully leverage the benefits of precision medicine.

InformedDNA Mission and Vision

InformedDNA is revolutionizing the application of genomic insights to enhance patient care and improve outcomes for all, shaping the future of precision healthcare.

Mission

We are revolutionizing the application of genomic insights to enhance patient care and improve outcomes for all.

Vision

To shape the future of precision healthcare.

This approach works because everybody on the team is then aligned and passionate about what they want the company to achieve and how they want to achieve it. After the off-site, the company belongs to everyone, not just the founder/CEO/family who started it. This is often the first time this broader group of management people has really been challenged to consider what the company is about and what it needs to do in order to achieve the goals that have been set.

We worked with one founder/CEO who *said* he was ready to share power and responsibility, but when it came time to actually do it, he wasn't able to. Eventually, he had to turn over the CEO position to someone who was ready to do what was required to grow the company.

It can be hard for the people who have been in charge to let go of some control and power, to share it with these managers, but it's essential that they do this if the company is going to transform and grow!

What to Consider during This Phase

This is the point with our partner companies at which it becomes clear to everyone that we can't realize our ambitious objectives without soliciting the full involvement, commitment, and productivity of every employee in the company. Everyone must buy into the Vision/ Mission/Purpose and Values/Behavior Statements. We need to clearly define and obtain agreement on the amazing opportunity for growth and profitability that has presented itself. Even with limitless opportunity, management will always face the challenge of executing against that opportunity with limited resources, so everyone involved must be fully engaged.

The three elements in the Vision/Mission/Purpose Statement are related, and we define them as follows:

- Vision is the destination of your company in the future—basically the image of the future that you worked out on the From-To Chart.

- Mission is how you will deliver on your vision—what you will actually do to get there.

- Purpose is why your company does this work—and it's very important for motivation that people know why they are doing what they're doing.

Sometimes, the effort to define these elements requires just a transitioning or tweaking of an existing Vision/Mission/Purpose Statement. In other cases, the effort takes a couple of days and multiple sessions to properly and effectively define—either because they've never been defined or because they need to change significantly to meet the new challenges the company faces. Whatever it takes, you must stick with this process until full agreement has been reached.

The same is true of the Values/Behavior Statement, which is an articulation of the values the company lives by and how those values are expressed overtly in working relationships within the company and interactions with customers and other stakeholders outside the company. Again, some may think this document is not essential, but investors are very interested in your values and behavior, because those establish that your company has the kind of culture that can deliver what is necessary to transform/grow. Combined with the Vision/Mission/Purpose Statement, this is what clearly defines the culture of your company and enables it to interest investors, motivate current employees, attract talented new employees who can put your plan into action, and draw customers to your products and services.

Here is an example of one company's way of describing itself before our off-site meeting and after it. Notice how much more direct and focused the second description is.

Why We Founded Catalyst
- Large chasm between clinical staffing services and full-service CROs
- Ability to work with the industry's best and brightest
- Ability to do what's right for clients
- To be a true value-added partner to our clients

Vision Statement
Build the dominant CRO provider for oncology pre-approval Clinical Development Services for smaller and midsize biopharma customers by:
- People-first culture
- Providing ethical, transparent, and high quality clinical trial planning and execution services
- Seeking out opportunities to innovate
- Passion and focus on driving better outcomes for all stakeholders

The Results of Success in This Phase

For a company that clearly establishes and then communicates to employees its vision, mission, purpose, values, and behavior, and gets commitment from its employees to all these elements, the possibilities for success are immense. I like to point to two companies that have achieved this to an extraordinary degree: Southwest Airlines and Chick-fil-A. In my view these companies do a great job of defining their business, mission, and values, articulating these things to their entire employee base, and motivating those employees to act on them.

Southwest has a different business model than most of the major airlines. Every employee understands their role in the most important objective of Southwest Airlines: keeping their airplanes in the air. To do this, their planes spend less time on the ground and more in the air than any other airline. Southwest does not generate revenue unless their airplanes are flying, and they have built a business model focused on that one factor, which allows them to produce additional flights per day per aircraft. They also use the same type of plane everywhere, too, which allows their pilots, ground crews, and maintenance people to be familiar with any plane they have to work with.

What has always struck me in my experiences with Southwest is that, regardless of where you are in the country—Baltimore, Nashville, San Diego, or wherever—you have the same experience with the people you deal with. Southwest uses the same check-in process, which is unique in the industry, everywhere. And, as those of you who have flown Southwest know, their employees do this while having fun, when they greet you at check-in or when the very engaging flight attendants serve you while in the air.

What is the business magic that enables this to happen? Somewhere in Southwest a strategy and set of values have been set, and everyone in the company is aligned with delivering on that strategy and acting on those values. For example—and I've actually seen this—if the baggage handlers are challenged with getting the bags on a plane quickly enough, which threatens on-time departure, you'll see other members of the Southwest team—including *pilots*—on the tarmac putting bags on the plane. Though it is not their job, the entire employee base understands that their corporate objective is to get those planes in the air as quickly as possible to generate revenue, which pays their salaries and bonuses. It's a great business model, but it's also a great example of the importance of articulating strategy and values and executing them in a focused and aligned way.

And, as I've mentioned previously, the secret to achieving this is having an engaged and committed middle management team, which is what we develop at our on-site by listening to everyone's input and getting them to commit to the goals and the system. It is the middle management team that translates your strategy and values into successful execution.

Chick-fil-A is another example of strategy and values permeating a company. No matter which store you visit, your experience is the same. The food is outstanding, the store is clean, and the employees you encounter are warm, kind, and completely focused on your satisfaction. How do they do it? Somewhere in Atlanta's corporate headquarters, values and a strategy have been set, and middle management translates them into flawless execution at every store—and this is a business where the employee base is mostly young people and turnover is high! Yet their performance is consistently excellent. I would argue again that the most important element of Chick-fil-A's success is that engaged middle management teams train and motivate the employees.

I also want to mention how deftly Chick-fil-A adapted to the challenges of the COVID-19 pandemic, which caused the demise of many restaurants. Chick-fil-A found a way to not be victimized by the pandemic; instead, they used it as an opportunity to transform the way their stores operated and continued to execute on their strategy and values.

The drive-through lines at Chick-fil-A—and every other fast-food restaurant—were enormously long during COVID-19, because no one could go into the stores. At other fast-food places, people just had to wait to get to the order kiosk or window. But Chick-fil-A sent employees out to the curb with tablet computers to take orders *and* payment, submitting orders much quicker than other fast-food restaurants. You could be the fifteenth car in a line, and suddenly a young man or woman would appear to take care of you, getting your order processed so that you received your food much quicker than you would have if you'd had to go all the way up to a kiosk or window. It was brilliant! And the employees executed it efficiently and cheerfully. Again, I would argue that this was achieved through the leadership of their middle management team, which bought in to this shift in business procedure and flawlessly communicated it to the people working for them.

Nick Dyer, Chairman of the Board and CEO of Catalyst, believes that a clear, strong culture is essential to success when using The Management System:

> I am a strong advocate for a very explicit, intentional culture, by which I mean the kind of behaviors we need to see among our employees to drive the kind of internal and external engagement that we want to achieve. Catalyst is a human capital company. It's a professional services organization that provides clinical trial support and leadership for our

clients. Our mission is to design and execute better clinical trials, and we do that with our expert teams aligned with technology. But the human element of this work is really important. And I don't feel that we would have a strong customer service ethos and a strong level of engagement if we didn't have a very intentional culture.

We did a lot of work around what behaviors and values we wanted to underpin our culture. And those values line up very neatly with the elements of The Management System. We believe in transparency, in listening in order to understand what we need to achieve, and in being committed to those achievements. And that's what the Tracking Sheets do: create transparency about the things that are important to us as an organization.

One of our other values is making agreements with one another and keeping our commitments. The Roles and Responsibilities Sheets support that by making sure that we understand who's accountable for what, who's responsible for actions and activities, and who depends on whom for what. When ambiguity around this arises, we go back to those Roles and Responsibilities Sheets and clarify things. That allows us to be very explicit about ownership, which drives accountability and strong commitment across the organization.

Clarifying Where You Are and Where You're Going

Two other important things we do at the off-site with our portfolio partners are (1) establish the specific True North goals against which all efforts will be measured, and (2) challenge management to be honest about where the company truly is at present—its strengths, weaknesses, opportunities, and threats. This is the SWOT Analysis I described in the last chapter. Let's begin with True North.

Finding True North

If the expectation for a company's next year's revenue, as agreed to by that company, is $100 million, that becomes the True North revenue objective. If that company's articulation of next year's EBITDA at $100 million in revenue is $30 million, that becomes the True North EBITDA objective. We all agree on the True North objectives for the upcoming year, and that is what we all direct our efforts toward achieving.

So, as we look toward the next operational or fiscal period, we have a defined revenue target and a defined EBITDA target. We also like True North goals to incorporate targets for employee and customer engagement. These goals represent a balanced scorecard focused on how the company will operationalize revenue growth, manage and operationalize EBITDA growth, fully engage employees, and ultimately meet or exceed customer satisfaction goals. If a company is able to operationalize the work of its employees and target them toward annual goals specifically tied to each of these four elements, it will be on the path to scalability and growth.

It is also important to note that if any member of the company's senior management team has a variable compensation element or bonus plan that is based on performance, it will be tied *directly* to their performance against the True North objectives. Any work or effort expended throughout the year not directly tied to impacting the True North goals is wasted. Pascal Dennis insists that it's all about getting the *right* work done. Companies that are at an inflection point of transformation/growth have limitless business opportunities and limited resources, so the management team is always faced with trade-offs concerning where resources should be expended. Defining True North goals is the starting point for an aligned management team and employee base, all focusing their energies on the most important work—the work that is going to achieve those goals.

As we will discuss in more detail later in the book, aligning everyone around the same objectives also reduces or eliminates the kind of politics and parochialism that can significantly inhibit a company's effectiveness and therefore its growth. Pursuing limitless opportunity is a matter of making the most effective use of the resources and assets that you have and making very quick decisions as you pursue that opportunity. There is no time for politics and parochialism as you pursue those goals—they will only impede your progress.

The Importance of an Honest SWOT Analysis

After completing the Vision/Mission/Purpose and Values/Behavior Statements as well as the From-To Chart and True North, it is important to have the current senior management team do a very honest SWOT Analysis. We challenge them to provide an assessment of their company's strengths, weaknesses, opportunities, and threats that characterize the company at the current moment. It is impossible to get somewhere else if you don't know exactly where you're starting from, what obstacles and challenges might prevent you from getting there, and what you have already that will help you on the journey.

The entire senior management team needs to contribute to the SWOT Analysis. We often find it helpful to break the senior management team into several groups to provide input into this analysis. This SWOT Analysis serves as a macroview of the company's position related to the market for which it has decided to compete. It also serves as a guide to ensure that the metrics that end up landing on the Tracking Sheets are established with a view on how to address the items listed on the SWOT Analysis.

Up to this point in our work with a partner company, we have:

- Defined and agreed on the company's vision/mission/purpose

- Defined the fundamental elements of the company's culture—its values and the behavior expected of leadership and employees

- Laid out a From-To Chart that specifically outlines what the company wants to look like in five years

- Laid out a specific set of operational targets, the company's True North, which comprises at least revenue and EBITDA for the next fiscal year and ideally includes employee engagement and customer engagement goals as well

- Performed a SWOT Analysis to establish the company's current state, what difficulties it will face, as well as what strengths it can rely on as everyone pursues the True North goals

This is all critical to getting any company on track at the point of inflection, and the next challenge is how to *operationalize* the entire organization to achieve the True North goals. It's now time to move to how the organization will do its work, where that work is to be performed within the organization, what the expectations are for each functional area, and how to measure whether each function is successful in doing its work. And, very importantly, you must ensure that *all the work* being done is directly aligned to the True North goals for the fiscal year. We will now move to The Management System elements that define this process: Functional Constructs and the Roles and Responsibilities and Tracking Sheets.

4

REDEFINING ROLES AND RESPONSIBILITIES

F or any company to successfully scale itself for growth, it is essential that there be a clear understanding of how the work of the company gets done. In an early-stage company, what we typically find is that the work performed is based on the priority of the moment. While this is completely acceptable for such a company, where resources are severely constrained, it is not acceptable for a company attempting to scale itself for growth. You cannot scale a company when the performance is solely dependent on a few key people in the company. You can only scale the company when the work is process-dependent, not people-dependent, and you're able to allocate your best talent to the work best suited for that talent.

At an early-stage company, everyone is jumping in on the critical task or the important priority of the week. The people involved may or may not have the skill set appropriate for that work, but they get involved anyway—usually because they are the only hands and minds available to do it. If your company is going to scale, you must match your people resources to the work where they can excel. When you're able to do that across all your work streams, you have positioned the company to scale successfully.

The Management System accomplishes this by establishing a Functional Construct for the business. On the surface, this sounds simple, but I find one of the most challenging parts of implementing the system to be when a company is transitioning from their early stage through their inflection point to the growth stage. The challenge is that the people in the company have been doing whatever is necessary in the moment to get the job done, but this approach will not enable them to reach the full potential of the company. So this is the moment where change must happen in the processes and in leadership attitudes.

Jeanne Hecht, CEO of JTH Consulting, who has worked with QHP and a number of our partner companies, tells the story of a CEO who enjoyed hiring people he liked and did this for roles such as business development, which was not his strong suit. He hired two business development people who didn't have the skill set the job demanded. Once the company clearly defined roles and responsibilities, the CEO was able to surrender this role to someone who understood what kind of people were needed in this function. And that new head of business development let go of the two people hired by the CEO and replaced them with people who could move the company forward.

There are many organizational structures that can be successful for various types of companies. However, at this moment, we want to focus only on how the work is done, not on an organizational structure. So one of the rules we establish as we work with companies on this particular task is that they can't talk about specific people in the company, because we want to be process-oriented, not people-oriented. They can't talk about organizational design, because we want to focus on defining the work itself and how that work needs to be done going forward. We have complete buy-in from everyone involved that there's a tremendous market opportunity, and we have complete buy-in about the fact that things need to change if the company is going to realize its full potential given that market opportunity. But it can be difficult when we get down to "inflicting" change on the company. However, this is a critical step in the successful deployment of The Management System.

The task is to break down the work into its functional elements, starting at the very beginning. I always ask management teams what the first thing is that has to happen in the company, and then what has to happen next. And after that, what's next? And then what? Overall, the work of the company is linear—there's a start and a finish (although some functions complement the linear work episodically).

What we do is break down the work into three high-level categories:

1. Enablement functions

2. Execution functions

3. Supporting functions

Here is a Functional Construct graphic that illustrates this:

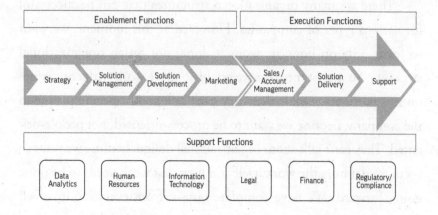

Let's look at each of these functional areas.

Enablement Functions

It is within the enablement functions that the work of any company starts. What industry are you going to serve? What market are you going to go after? How are you going to position yourself in the market? And so on. Their functions determine the work the company will do—answering the kinds of questions I just posed and directing the execution functions of the company. Enablement functions are responsible for bringing your company's solutions to the market. At a high level, they comprise these four work functions: strategy, solution management, solution development, and marketing.

In enablement function work streams, all decisions are made relative to how the company is going to position itself in the market and what it must do to succeed in that market. In an early-stage company, such decisions have been made mostly by the founder and the early team, who made them on the basis of their own experience and their outstanding intuition. But as a company moves through an inflection point and has to scale itself in order to grow, it must more carefully consider and think through such decisions, and that is the job of these functions. They will direct all the resources of the company going forward.

This is what each of these enablement functions is responsible for:

- **Strategy**: Determines what segments of the market you will go after

- **Solution management**: Ensures that the solution is fit for the chosen market

- **Solution development**: Constructs the solution that will be marketed (this is an enablement function, rather than an execution function, because it does not in itself generate revenue—products are worthless in a business sense until they are actually sold to customers and customers start using them)

- **Marketing**: Prepares the market for the solutions and builds demand for them

Execution Functions

These functions take direction from the enablement work streams and are responsible for transacting the business of the company with its customers. They are the foot soldiers, the folks "in the trenches" who actually deliver and maintain the solutions. The execution functions are sales, implementation, services, and customer support. Here is what each of these functions is responsible for:

- **Sales/account management**: Finds leads and converts suspects and prospects into customers and manages customers' needs

- **Solution delivery and services**: Delivers and implements the solutions for the customer and provides all the services that go along with the solutions, including training, operational support, consulting, and so on

- **Support**: Resolves customer issues and ensures customer satisfaction

When you lay the enablement functions and the execution functions side by side, they define in linear fashion the totality of the work a company does. This linear representation of the work is important because it lays the foundation for defining what particular work tasks belong within each specific function—and, equally important, what work tasks do not belong with that function. It also defines which are upstream functions that are responsible for delivering their output to downstream function. It is critical to fully define the relationships between functions, and I'll say more about this later.

Supporting Functions

The supporting functions represent work that is required to help both the enablement and execution functions be successful. Where the work of the enablement and execution functions is linear and systematic, the work of supporting functions is often episodic, meaning that their services are employed on an "as-needed basis," although some of these functions also have ongoing duties that serve the company as a whole.

Supporting functions include:

- **Human resources**: Manages the rights and benefits of employees as well as their hiring and separation

- **Information technology**: Ensures that each function has the technological tools it needs to do its work effectively

- **Legal**: Writes and administers contracts and deals with any legal questions or issues that arise

- **Finance**: Manages the company's money and provides data on revenue, expenditures, tax obligations, and so on

- **Compliance/quality**: Ensures compliance with both company and industry quality and compliance standards

- **Facilities**: Maintains all aspects of the physical plant

The role of supporting functions is to assist the prioritized activity of the enablement and execution functions as well as assist the totality of the business in various ways. Some of this work is ongoing, and some of it is episodic. To give an example of episodic work, if your company entered its new growth phase with too small a sales organization, it would have to build a larger sales organization, and that would be done with the help of human resources. The sales function would depend on human resources for a period of time to assist in hiring talented individuals for its expanded sales organization. And if, at the same time, the finance function was not hiring, there would be no relationship between the human resources function and the finance function in this area. These are the kinds of episodic relationships that supporting functions enter into with enablement and execution functions.

As I've said, the human resources department also engages in ongoing company-wide activities, such as performance management, benefits, selections, overall personnel management, etc. But in the context of prosecuting the actual work of the company, as defined within the Functional Construct of enablement and execution, those relationships are episodic, depending on the priority of the business.

Assigning Roles and Responsibilities to Each Function

Every company is different, so how they define their specific work functions within the enablement, execution, and supporting functions will also be different. It matters not how you define them, but it does matter that the entire senior management team agrees to these definitions. Once you have the Functional Construct built and agreed upon, you must now define what you mean by each function, and what specific work is done within each function. Here we use a tool that is referred to as the Roles and Responsibilities Sheet and work with the team to define roles and responsibilities for each function. Again, the entire team works on this, and they must reach an agreement before we can go on.

There is a very specific rule that I developed over the years as I worked with companies to define what belongs on the Roles and Responsibilities Sheets: if there is a specific work task that is important to accomplish, it must land on *one* specific Roles and Responsibilities Sheet and must not be listed on any other Roles and Responsibilities Sheets. The task simply cannot land on multiple sheets.

It is particularly challenging to define things this clearly for companies that have been very people-dependent, with their priorities shifting from week to week depending on the CEO/founder or a few key members of the management team. This approach has often whiplashed employees, forcing them to respond to the priority of the moment and distracting them from their primary work tasks. So you end up with a few heroes of the company while the remainder of the employee base is confused, disenfranchised, and not as productive as they could be if their roles and responsibilities were clear.

This is an important step toward moving the company from a people-dependent organization to a process-dependent organization, which will enable the company to scale its efforts and grow. I often take this moment at the off-sites to drive home this point by asking the management team: Which function owns revenue? Or, which function owns EBITDA? Usually, several functions say that they own these things. But revenue and EBITDA cannot land on multiple Roles and Responsibilities Sheets; important metrics must land on just one sheet, so it's clear who has responsibility for them.

Each function must articulate clearly what they are responsible for. Their Roles and Responsibilities Sheet must include the following elements:

- **Role definition**: A high-level, simple sentence or two articulating the function

- **Responsibilities**: The specific major work activities exclusive to this function

- **Dependencies**: What the function is dependent on in order to deliver its work

- **Accountabilities**: The specific outputs that are to be delivered by this function as a result of doing their work

- **Decision rights**: The specific decisions that can be made only within this function and for which they are accountable

- **Skill requirements**: The specific skills that are required by employees to perform the work of this function

It's not that the companies we work with have been unable to make decisions about who they need where, or which roles and responsibilities they need to fill. They've just been reluctant to make investments in some areas because they haven't had a framework to help them see the effectiveness of those investments. They haven't been clear about the results that they could derive from those investments. So establishing these Roles and Responsibilities Sheets lays the foundation for how they're going to measure success as they do their work.

The Importance of This Work

At QHP, we do this work of defining functions, roles, and responsibilities with that middle management team as part of our one-week off-site before The Management System is put into place. At this off-site, everyone is effectively equal—perhaps for the first time. The executives in the room represent the broad middle management team that will be the key to the success of the company going forward, so it is a critical step to define the work of the company in such a way that every one of these executives agrees to it—not only to the definitions of the work, but to the specific work that rests within their particular function.

Again, this represents a very challenging part of the process because we are there to change how their business has been done to how to it will be done going forward. So each of the individuals on the middle management team must agree to change the way they work, which is not easy. Not that what we come up with at the off-site is final. This is an interactive process, because the company continues to learn how to best define its work in a way that will give it the highest possible probability of success.

During the off-site, we have to have all the discussion and debate necessary to decide where responsibilities lie and where decisions are to be made. One way of avoiding "turf wars" during this process is by foregoing talk about specific people, the way things have been done, or any particular system for doing things. We must convince people at the off-site that this is essential for changing the way the company works in order to scale and grow.

When you define the work through a linear expression of the enablement and execution functions, you're effectively looking at processes, not people. With all processes, in order to make them efficient, you want as few steps and as few layers of structure as possible to create efficient workflow. That is exactly what we do at the off-site: we go through the effort to define the Functional Construct and the roles and responsibilities of each function.

With The Management System, we attempt to drive decision-making as deep into the organization as possible. We do this because it enhances productivity and success. But for the core management and former owner/family/member entrepreneur who has been running the company, this process of redefinition can bring significant discomfort because they have essentially been making all the decisions up until this point.

Ashton Poole, a QHP Partner, has seen this more than once:

> It's not easy for the founder-owner to let go of things they've been doing since they started the company. They had to do it because everybody needed to take on multiple roles. But when they know they've got a framework like the Roles and Responsibilities Sheets, it allows for accountability. The Tracking Sheet reviews allow them to keep an eye on the function they've handed off. This gives the confidence to delegate, because they're going to know whether or not the delegation is working—and if it isn't, they can make adjustments as needed.

As Ashton indicates, Tracking Sheets, which we'll discuss next, can ultimately provide some comfort to these leaders, because these sheets define accountability for the results of the work and for the decision-making that is being more widely dispersed. But before they can work on the Tracking Sheets, a company must first go through the difficult and challenging task of creating the very specific Roles and Responsibilities Sheets and agree on them.

Once this process is complete, each manager will be assigned to a functional area and have a clear definition of what their role is, what the work requirements of their function are, what they are dependent on to get that work done, and what they're expected to produce as a result of doing their work. They will also, very importantly, have clarity regarding the decisions that they can make in the context of doing that work. When we design the Tracking Sheets for these functions, which is how the company is going to track the execution of their work, it creates a transparency that builds a culture of trust and accountability. And when the functional leadership is being responsible and accountable across all functions, that is where the magic happens. That is where companies find that they can scale and scale rapidly, achieving a level of success far beyond their current state.

I mentioned the importance of the decision-making factor, and I'd like to underline that. A company can only be great when it's operating frictionlessly across functions. And to drive that frictionless execution across the whole company, each execution function's decision-making must be driven deep into those functions. It is incredibly inefficient to constantly have to go up and down the hierarchy of an organizational structure to get decisions made. Those decisions need to be made as close to the work—as close to the customer—as possible, and that is from within and across the functions, not from higher up in the organizational structure.

When each function is performing its individual tasks in an efficient and effective manner while operating efficiently and effectively across functions, delivering on their responsibilities, and getting what they need from other functions to do their work, then you're on the way to creating a great organization. As everyone learns more and more about how the organization works, and where the levers are to get things done, they'll become even more efficient at how they work together and how they make decisions.

Mike Raymer, CEO of Pro-ficiency, has seen the value of this knowledge over several companies he's led:

> What is critical about the functional workflows is that they allow everyone to see how they fit into the organization and what their dependencies are, both up and downstream within the organization. The Roles and Responsibilities Sheets are somewhat similar to job descriptions, but instead of just focusing on one job description, they comprise a functional job description for each function and, cumulatively, for the entire organization. This makes it so much easier to hire people to scale functions, because people know immediately what they need to do. And if something isn't getting done, you go back to the Roles and Responsibilities Sheets and identify the workflow gap. The transparency is great. The sheets are available to anyone, and they allow people to see what the workflow is for their own function and for any other function.

Understanding the implications of performing your function and the performance of other functions, and how they relate to one another, produces real understanding of the business. This understanding allows the organization to quickly deal with challenges and take advantage of new opportunities. You learn more about what moves the needle in your business and how to drive optimal performance.

With everyone on the senior management team and middle management team understanding how the work is done, where the work is done, and how the work is measured, you have a solid framework for scalability.

QHP Partner Matt Jenkins describes how this approach empowers people:

> I have seen how the establishment of clearly defined roles through The Management System really unlocks great potential in people. Some colleagues come to work every day and want to be told what to do, what to deliver, etc. The Roles and Responsibilities Sheets are good for them, because these people get clarity on what is expected of them with consistency day to day. However, there are also people in almost every company and at all levels of the organization who care tremendously about both the company and their own individual performance and get burned out. These highly talented people are often overextended, or they wear too many hats. When we rescope their job together and give them clarity, it is often very refreshing. Clarity of scope and expectations reduces the confusion and political infighting these very engaged people have to deal with. Because they're not spending time fighting with their peers over organization scope and are clear on their role, it allows them to focus and spend their energies driving results. They have the power to make decisions and do what they think is necessary, as long as they deliver on the metrics they've agreed to. We often get people who may have been stuck in low-level or middle management roles whose potential is unlocked through the process. They reach a level of individual potential they would not have without the clarity of this system.

As a final side note, having developed the Functional Construct and defined it in detail via the Roles and Responsibilities Sheets, you will have created a phenomenal tool to help you if you decide to assimilate an acquisition, create a partnership, or determine a technology dependency to support your business. At QHP, we have had many experiences with companies integrating an acquisition by using the Functional Construct and Roles and Responsibilities Sheets to compare how the work is done in their company with how it is done in the company being acquired. This quickly identifies gaps in processes and capability differences and helps prioritize what must be done to completely and successfully integrate and operationalize the acquired company.

Mike Raymer, CEO of Pro-ficiency, who I quoted above, has had direct experience using the Roles and Responsibilities Sheets in an acquisition process:

> Last year we acquired Fugitive Labs, which built out the technical side of our organization. And, coming into our organization, every new manager was able to see their functional workflow clearly defined, and they were pleased to see so clearly how what they did would fit in with what we were doing. We were able to start with the Roles and Responsibilities Sheets and identify where there were unique things that they did that complemented what we did, where they fit functionally, and where there would be cross-functional dependencies. It made the merging of the two companies much more efficient.

In the next chapter, I'll go into more detail about how clearly and transparently The Management System enables you to track per-

formance and profitability as you scale the company and pursue your
True North goals.

5

TRACKING YOUR PERFORMANCE

Earlier, I told the story of my experience as the new CEO of Misys Healthcare, when, after being there for a month, I came into my office suite to find twelve thick, white three-ring binders piled onto my conference table. They turned out to be the monthly reports from each business unit in the company. One was fifty pages long, another seventy, and so on, and they were filled with graphs, spreadsheets, narratives, and endless metrics. I didn't know anyone who could process that much information quickly enough to make decisions that would help the company prosper and grow. We needed a strategy shift, a transformation that would get us focused on the work that was *really* important and on the *handful* of metrics that would allow us to determine whether we were on track for success. It was at this moment that The Management System was born.

As I looked at the overwhelming amount of information in those binders, it was clear to me that there was a lot of reporting going on in the company but very little real managing of the business. With our current approach, there was no way any of us could stay on top of the execution and operation of the business, on top of our competitive pressures and market conditions, and make appropriate business decisions. The key to doing those things effectively was focus and alignment. Focus meant that we needed to spend our energy on the most important metrics tied to our performance. Alignment meant that everyone needed to agree on how we were going to do that. We needed a system that would allow us to create focus and alignment across an organization that needed to transform quickly.

I've described the way The Management System defines how work is done in a company and the roles and responsibilities of each function required to get that work done. Now we must turn our attention to how The Management System *measures* whether you are performing according to your plan—and if your plan needs to be adjusted. And if the plan does need to be adjusted, how do you ensure that everyone is focused and aligned to that adjustment? In The Management System, the primary tool for accomplishing this is the Tracking Sheet.

How the Tracking Sheet Works

Below is a sample of a Tracking Sheet, the tool that enables companies to keep on top of their goals and uncover problems as soon as they occur. The first thing you need to know about the Tracking Sheet is that all its metrics must be aligned to your company's True North. From a private equity perspective, this is the revenue and EBITDA that we "buy" when we negotiate a partnership with a company. You can also look at it as your revenue and EBITDA goal for the fiscal period. With a balanced scorecard approach, like the one shown in the sample, True North comprises the annual revenue goal, the annual EBITDA goal, and a customer satisfaction and employee engagement target. (I have also seen bookings added as a fifth objective.) Not every Tracking Sheet for functional areas can accomplish this balanced metric approach, but that should be the goal.

TRUE NORTH

KPIs	FY Plan	Actual/FC	% of Target
Net Revenue	$ 409,000,000	$ 418,303,060	100%
Adjusted EBITDA	$ 145,000,000	$ 146,740,771	90%
Customer NPS	-70	14	90%
Colleague NPS	30	32	100%

CEO - Rollup
Fiscal Year - 2023

	KPI	Measurement	Prior Period	Target	Variance	Jan	Feb	Mar	Apr	May	Jun	Jul	Aug	Sep	Oct	Nov	Dec	2023
Financial	Net Revenue	Gross Revenue - Consolidated GTN	$374,000,000	$409,000,000	Plan	$ 32,000,000	$ 32,000,000	$ 32,000,000	$ 33,000,000	$ 33,000,000	$ 33,000,000	$ 34,000,000	$ 34,000,000	$ 34,000,000	$ 36,000,000	$ 38,000,000	$ 38,000,000	$ 409,000,000
					Act / FC	$ 33,402,580	$ 37,246,005	$ 35,203,607	$ 34,108,744	$ 35,227,601	$ 32,645,102	$ 33,126,538	$ 33,112,312	$ 37,401,357	$ 36,234,435	$ 33,402,604	$ 36,391,163	$ 418,303,060
					MTD (QTD) +/-	$ 1,402,580	$ 5,246,005	$ 3,203,607	$ 1,108,744	$ 2,227,601	$ (354,898)	$ (834,442)	$ (687,688)	$ 3,401,357	$ 734,435	$ (4,097,396)	$ (1,608,835)	$ 9,303,060
					YTD +/-	$ 1,402,580	$ 6,648,585	$ 9,852,192	$ 10,960,936	$ 13,188,537	$ 12,833,639	$ 11,999,197	$ 11,311,509	$ 14,712,866	$ 15,447,301	$ 11,349,905	$ 9,741,060	$ 9,301,060
	Adjusted EBITDA	Net Revenue - Consolidated Expenses	$130,000,000	$145,000,000	Plan	$ 10,000,000	$ 10,000,000	$ 10,000,000	$ 11,000,000	$ 11,000,000	$ 11,000,000	$ 12,000,000	$ 12,000,000	$ 12,000,000	$ 14,000,000	$ 16,000,000	$ 16,000,000	$ 145,000,000
					Act / FC	$ 10,775,103	$ 11,241,315	$ 10,689,209	$ 11,389,840	$ 9,189,405	$ 13,670,768	$ 10,363,728	$ 14,020,926	$ 9,512,421	$ 13,217,303	$ 11,126,073	$ 9,484,086	$ 135,280,771
					MTD +/-	$ 775,103	$ 1,241,315	$ 689,209	$ 389,844	$ (1,811,(4?)50)	$ 2,670,768	$ (1,636,272)	$ 2,020,926	$ (2,387,579)	$ (782,697)	$ (4,873,927)	$ (6,515,920)	$ (9,219,229)
					YTD +/-	$ 775,103	$ 2,017,018	$ 2,706,227	$ 3,096,067	$ 1,284,922	$ 3,955,640	$ 2,319,368	$ 4,340,294	$ 1,952,715	$ 3,170,018	$ 1,703,955	$ (8,211,229)	$ (10,438,459)
Operational	Earnings Per Share	Net Income / Common Share Outstanding	$3.25	$3.60	Plan			3.25			3.35		3.48		3.50		3.60	3.60
					Act / FC			3.34			3.41		3.50		3.50		3.30	3.30
					MTD +/-			0.09			0.06		0.02		3.50		(0.30)	(0.30)
	SG&A % or Revenue	Non-Capitalized Expenses	38%	35%	Plan	38%	38%	38%	37%	37%	37%	36%	36%	36%	35%	35%	35%	35%
					Act / FC	37%	36%	37%	37%	35%	34%	40%	32%	36%	37%	46%	43%	43%
					MTD +/-	1%	2%	1%	0%	2%	3%	4%	4%	2%	2%	-11%	8%	8%
Customer	Customer NPS	NPS for Sample of All Customers	-70	10	Plan			-50			-30		-10		30		10	10
					Act / FC			40			30		30		30		10	10
					MTD +/-			-10			-30		-10				10	10
Colleague	Colleague NPS	NPS for All Colleagues	30	30	Plan			30			30		30		30		30	30
					Act / FC			30			30		30		30		30	30
					MTD +/-			0			0		0				30	30

You may have noticed that there is not a huge number of metrics to track—we're a long way from those thick, white binders full of data! To keep Tracking Sheets as succinct as possible, I came up with The Rule of 10. There can be only ten or fewer of the most important metrics for each function for the year on a Tracking Sheet. You must determine the critically important metrics that are required from each of your functional organizations to achieve its True North objectives. And yes, it is a challenge to narrow down the most important objectives to ten, but this is a critical exercise *for the entire management team* to engage in. It is not just up to each function to make that determination alone. I always engage the entire senior management team in the discussion about the most important metrics for each function because these metrics indicate what the organization feels it needs from each function in order to achieve the whole company's True North goals. This process does a great job of aligning the organization, because everyone is providing input as to what is most important for *every* function, not just their own.

The ten metrics you come up with for each function must include the financial, operational, employee, and customer metrics that best represent the most important work being performed by that function for the operating year. The metrics on the Tracking Sheet must directly reflect the output of that function as defined on its Roles and Responsibilities Sheet, and they must define an operational plan for that function across all twelve months of the operating year.

A Tracking Sheet incorporates:

- The metric itself

- The metric definition

- How the metric is measured

- If the metric was tracked in the previous year and, if so, what the previous year's performance was

- The goal for that metric for the current operating year

- The specific performance metric for each month of the operating year

Now let's study the Tracking Sheet example provided.

- The left-most column represents the four **metrics being tracked**: financial, operational, employee satisfaction, and customer satisfaction.

- The next column is the **key performance indicator** (KPI). This is one of the top ten metrics for this Tracking Sheet.

- Next you'll see the measurement, **how the metric is being calculated**. A good practice when using an Excel-based Tracking Sheet is to put a comment with that cell that says exactly where the data is being sourced and the calculation that is being computed for the metric. It's important that anyone in the organization be able to look at the Tracking Sheet and understand exactly what's going on for each metric.

- The next column, Prior Period, shows **if this metric was tracked in the prior fiscal year**, and if it was, the performance result is indicated.

- The Target column shows your plan for the current fiscal period—your **goal for this metric for the full year**.

- The January through December columns **divide the annual metric into goals for each month**. Each of the cells will have a specific target for that month, which is the way you express how you expect the year to unfold for that metric. In some cases, the metric may be the same for every month, because the expectation is that the metric will be consistent every month. However, in the case of some metrics, such as revenue, there may be seasonal differences, such as a heavy fourth quarter, a light early year, etc. The management team must use its best judgment to express how they expect this metric to perform for each month. Setting this plan in place allows the team to not only focus on that objective, but to also understand how the business performs throughout the year and make adjustments when things do not go according to plan.

- When you get to the operational objective of **earnings per share**, you see another interesting element of the Tracking Sheet. Earnings per share is a metric measured quarterly in the case of public companies, and you can see that this metric is planned on a quarterly basis and that the first two months of each quarter are grayed out because there is no metric or measurement for earnings per share in those months.

- **Customer NPS** (customer satisfaction) and **Colleague NPS** (employee satisfaction) are also not measured monthly on this sheet.

- The last column of the Tracking Sheet represents the **full-year performance plan** for each of the metrics. Using a combination of your actual and forecasted performance, you can always tell how you're performing against the most important metrics by looking at the monthly performance of each.

In this example, I have chosen a simple CEO Tracking Sheet of my own, showing the most important objectives across the organization that I wanted to see as a CEO. In this case, there are six objectives in the KPI column: two financial, two operational, one customer satisfaction, and one employee satisfaction. As you look at the revenue objective, you can see that each month of the year has a plan number inserted into the Planned cell for each month. This represents how the management team believes the year will unfold relative to its revenue performance and how the organization should be planning for how each function should perform relative to revenue generation. The result of achieving this revenue objective will fulfill the obligation of exceeding one of the True North metrics—in this case, revenue.

As you look at the revenue objective throughout the year, you will see that for the months of January and February, the actual revenue performance of the company exceeded the monthly plan for revenue by three additional sales for each month, which resulted in higher-than-projected revenues. There are only two colors that represent results for a metric: green, which means that you met or exceeded your plan, and red, which indicates that things did not go according to plan. In the case of revenue on this sheet, you can see that we made our plan for January, February, and March and are in a very comfortable position as we exit the first quarter.

There is no yellow on the Tracking Sheet! Conversations around justifications for why we *almost* made a number or how some extraneous event impacted our performance are irrelevant. You either make your plan or you don't, and then you adjust accordingly.

One other significant benefit of using a Tracking Sheet is the ability to forecast. Looking at the revenue metric on the sample sheet, you can see that the cells of April and beyond are blue, which means that they represent a forecast for those future months. This allows functional executives to really understand their business and be able to project their expectations of future performance. In this case, you can see that when we get to June, our forecast does not achieve our planned objective. What was very useful to me as a CEO about being able to forecast future monthly performance was that I got to see whether the company would stay on plan for each metric. We are also seeing challenges in June, July, and August—and what's important is that we're seeing them early, at the end of March, based on our plan and our forecast. This means that the company could start making adjustments immediately based on our analysis of what is causing our performance to be short of the plan for that period.

So as the CEO—or any other executive in the company—you can be sitting in the back of the room at an operating committee meeting, look at a Tracking Sheet displayed on a screen and, seeing just the colors, determine the specific areas on which the function reporting needs to focus to make its goals. If a metric is green, of course, no action is required. But if a metric is red, the function must present an A3 (which I will say more about shortly) to define the action plan to get that metric back on track.

This is called management by exception, which allows you to focus both on the areas that are not going according to plan and the areas for which opportunities have arisen because the results exceed the goal, and you can accelerate your plan. I particularly love the transparency of the Tracking Sheet because management teams that successfully deploy them develop a deep understanding of how the company works, where the levers of performance are, and how to allocate resources in response to market or competitive dynamics.

The Tracking Sheet in Action

Mike Raymer, currently the CEO of Pro-ficiency, has employed The Management System at several companies, and here is what he says about the usefulness of Tracking Sheet presentations:

At our monthly reviews, we are able to go through all the Tracking Sheets, which map to the critical things that each functional area needs to do. We can go from the top to the bottom of the organization in three hours or less! This provides a really streamlined way to get an overall assessment of how the organization is performing each month. And it eliminates "grandstanding," the attempt to look good no matter what is happening in your area of the company. That happened in every business review I'd been in before I started using Tracking Sheets, because no one likes to talk about anything that's not going well. Most of the managers would wax poetic about all the things that went great and gloss over the things that didn't go well. Tracking Sheets don't allow you to do that. They enable you to quickly celebrate the wins, but they also acknowledge the areas where the organization needs to improve—and then we work on those problems together.

I encourage companies to use Tracking Sheets as the basis for a monthly operating committee meeting, where all the executives leading the functions come together to review all the Tracking Sheets. This has many inherent benefits, including directly affecting the company's performance.

The first benefit is that no functional executive wants to come to a monthly meeting of peers and show metrics that are not performing according to plan. The whole team is compensated based on the company's True North goals, so having a function that is not performing is problematic for everyone. Each functional executive wants to present their function and the performance of their function in the most positive way, but if what they're presenting is just blowing smoke—which, as Mike Raymer noted, I've seen people do time and time again in operating committee meetings—no one understands what's really going on. Tracking Sheets require executives to report in a transparent, fact-based way, not in a way that's based on a biased attempt to present their function's performance in the best light.

As I described earlier, at the off-site where The Management System is introduced, the entire management team gets together to determine the most important objectives for each function and agrees on them. So when the team comes together as an operating committee to review Tracking Sheets, they're reviewing what they all agreed were the most important metrics for the business, the metrics critical to executing in the way that will meet or exceed True North objectives for the year. If the reporting is honest and transparent, when a problem arises, the whole team can work together to solve it.

Red on a Tracking Sheet is not necessarily bad! This is a very important concept for functional executives to understand. Red is not a judgment; it's an indicator—it points out a situation that needs to be dealt with. Joanna Williams, a founder and now COO of Lexitas Pharma Services, describes the attitude that must be developed about seeing red on a Tracking Sheet:

> What we had to learn was to not look at red on the Tracking Sheet as good or bad, to not think that it's about the person reporting. It doesn't mean that the person has done something wrong. It's a problem with the business that needs to be examined, understood, and solved. It took people a while to get used to the idea that they could come to the operating committee meeting with red on their sheet and not be accused of doing something wrong, of failing. We're not there to say, "What did you do wrong?" It's more like, "Why are we not hitting this target? What's going on? Is it something in the industry? Is it something a client did? Is

it something that we can change or not? Or do we just have a bad target?" The goal is just to help you identify where your problems are so you can fix them—sometimes on your own and sometimes with the help of other functions.

A second significant benefit of the operating committee Tracking Sheet presentations is that the whole management team is continually seeing how the entire company works end to end. They're engaging in a discussion about the performance of *each* function, not just their own, and they're learning about the operational and financial leverage achieved by each of these functions working together. This increases the business acumen and the management judgment skills of every executive in the organization, and it leverages the combined expertise and experience of the entire management team. I've seen it over and over again as management teams sit together month after month: they see how every business function is performing; they're engaging in discussions of opportunities that can be capitalized on; they're confronting problems to be solved and metrics to be adjusted; and they're understanding the results of the decisions they make. Everyone improves their management skills as they better understand how the company works and how it performs across the entirety of the Functional Construct.

Again, I want to note that The Management System removes politics and parochialism from decision-making. It's a practical, cooperative effort. Each functional executive presents their top ten metrics, describes what's happening in their function, articulates the challenges they're anticipating, and engages the entire team in dealing with those challenges. The committee looks honestly at just the ten most important metrics—not thirty or forty or fifty, just ten, the ten that the entire team has determined are the most important. I have never seen an organization that achieved the metrics they chose to put on their Tracking Sheets for each function that did not succeed in achieving their True North objectives.

It is challenging at the beginning to determine what the most important metrics are and whether you can even measure them. And if you look at the metrics in six months and they don't make sense, you change them. The only thing that cannot change in The Management System is True North. This system is predicated on getting the right things done. If you sit in the operating committee meeting and need to adjust your plan or reprioritize metrics based on a business opportunity or challenge, then you do so.

Ed Seguine, former CEO and Board Advisor at Clinical Ink, describes how an adjustment in a Tracking Sheet metric uncovered a mysterious problem with on-time delivery of its products:

> In clinical trials, the First Patient First Visit date is among the most important milestones—all implementation activities are based on this key date. Consequently, "On-Time Shipping" was a key Tracking Sheet metric to ensure that all study materials arrived at the clinical trial sites on time. Despite an On-Time *Shipping* rate of 85 percent, our study materials were still not making it *to the research sites* on time. At the December Tracking Sheet meeting, the management team redefined the metric as "On-Time Delivery."
>
> At the next Tracking Sheet meeting, the "On-Time Delivery" metric showed that only 65 percent of deliveries were actually reaching the study sites on time. The most significant decision influenced by this metric was to insource our outsourced fulfillment activities because the outsource partner did not have expertise in international customs/import regulations, so many shipments sent out

on time were ultimately held up due to inaccurate/incomplete import documentation. This required a completely new department to be staffed and new facilities secured and optimally configured to handle our rapidly expanding volume. This solution, brought to light by finding the right Tracking Sheet metric, solved our delivery problem.

A lot of personal and professional growth happens across the entirety of the management team as a result of their participation and engagement in these operating committee meetings. They understand their business better as a result of understanding the metrics that drive their particular function. They understand the benefits that can be derived from working effectively across functions, understanding how performance in one function affects the performance of another. For example, if you have a great sales quarter, you must ensure that you have delivery personnel who can implement the solutions that have been sold. The better you get at forecasting and delivering, the better the downstream organizations can get at preparing and executing, resulting in enhanced utilization, better financial performance, and significant productivity to the organization.

Dealing with Red Metrics

The Management System is a transparent, fact-based system. It is solely based on objective measures of performance, not subjective ones, driving functional bias, politics, and parochialism out of the management decision-making. Your plan needs to represent your team's best judgment of how the business is going to perform throughout the operating year. It's your plan. And because there is no subjectivity allowed in The Management System, there is no subjectivity allowed in representing your performance against your plan.

I hate PowerPoint presentations of performance. They are inevitably filled with the bias of the leader and the parochialism of the function presenting, and they are rooted in some internal political agenda—but very rarely do they ever represent the *reality* of how the function is performing. Management can deal with facts, but it's very difficult to deal with subjective presentations. Tracking Sheets are different. If a function didn't make its plan, it didn't make its plan, and what's important is that you understand why a metric is red and articulate a plan of action that will turn it green, that you're clear about the work that needs to be done and implement that work as soon as possible.

With one company using The Management System, business consultant Jeanne Hecht experienced an executive who took advantage of Tracking Sheet metrics that didn't provide the most important information:

> The head of human resources would come to the monthly ops committee meeting and present her Tracking Sheet, and everything would be green, so it looked like she was doing her job perfectly. But hiring was not actually going well. The company wasn't getting the kind of new hires they needed. The people who depended on her were angry because they felt like she didn't have a sense of urgency when it came to hiring. But when you looked at her metrics, it looked like everything was going well. And what was happening was that she wasn't tracking the *right* metrics.
>
> For example, she was tracking the number of people hired on a monthly basis. So let's just say we had to hire twenty people over three months. She would say I need to hire six, six, and eight over the next three months. And she would

hire six people in the first month, six in the second, and eight in the third, so her metric would be green—but, in fact, she had hired the *wrong* six people. So she didn't hire the new hires the company actually needed in January, and instead hired people who were needed for March. She needed a metric that specified the kind of people she needed to hire each month, not just a number.

Unfortunately, some people think of metrics as a report card, and they always want to show green. But you don't get fired over your metrics. They're just intended to make sure that the business is functioning well. And, out of insecurity, some people try to game the system.

It's important that the metrics you establish are the right ones, and that you keep an eye on them and adjust them if they're not.

I've always thought that listening to explanations about why something was *almost* on target or was in *a range of acceptability* is wasted time. What is needed is not an elaborate explanation of why a target wasn't hit, but a plan to get it back on target—the past is history. The management team gets to decide where it's going to spend its time relative to all the metrics that are not performing according to plan. You need to spend your collective time on the most significant metrics, working through A3s to put a plan in place that will return the metric to a satisfactory performance level.

In my experience, there are three primary reasons that a metric is in the red:

1. Invalid assumptions when setting the plan

2. Execution

3. Leadership

Let's look at each of these elements.

1. **Invalid assumptions**: The best recent example of how planning assumptions can become invalid is the impact of COVID-19. No one could have planned for COVID-19 in the first quarter of 2020. Most of the companies we worked with had operationalized their 2020 plan in late 2019, and therefore went into 2020 with their roles and responsibilities in place and their Tracking Sheets organized to perform against a reasonable 2020 target. Then COVID-19 hit and changed everything. Hardly any assumption that was made across these companies was relevant anymore. Their Tracking Sheets were based on assumptions that were now invalid. The beauty of The Management System is that it has a framework in place for making necessary adjustments rapidly.

    Many companies were victimized by COVID-19. They weren't able to respond to the business challenges that appeared so suddenly. But other companies adjusted quickly. Having The Management System, with its monthly Tracking Sheet reviews, allows you to make adjustments nimbly when unexpected business challenges arise. It allows you to immediately operationalize according to new performance metrics tied to those adjustments.

2. **Execution**: The team is unable to execute the plan. There can be many reasons why this happens. For example, the sales function may not have enough salespeople hired to meet a bookings challenge, or the training function has not trained enough people to enable successful execution, or unexpected turnover is hampering the company's efforts. These are all

circumstances that can be changed if a lack of creativity or domain knowledge is recognized.

3. **Leadership**: The strategy is right, and the assumptions are valid. The team's function is executing based on their roles, responsibilities, and direction. But their leadership is not stepping up to the challenge in some way, such as not providing the resources to get the job done, not empowering the function to make key decisions, or not recognizing cross-functional problems.

It will help you begin to decipher why a metric is red if you first try to determine if the problem falls into one of these three most common categories, which will then make it easier to determine the action needed to get the metric back on plan.

The next step is to align the company horizontally and vertically with The Management System in order to execute effectively against your goals.

6

ENSURING ALIGNMENT

We've now reached a point where it's time to operationalize The Management System, as all the fundamental components have been put in place. To review:

- We started off the articulation of strategy in the form of a From-To Statement, which outlined a vision of where the company is today and where we want it to go in the future. Everyone involved has agreed on the future path and is committed to achieving this vision.

- We complemented that by developing a Vision/Mission/Purpose Statement and a Values/Behavior Statement for the company, which is the foundation for the all-important culture that needs to be in place to succeed and grow.

- The SWOT Analysis followed, an evaluation of the company in the context of today, outlining the strengths, weaknesses, opportunities, and threats—a macroview of the company in the context of the market, the competition, and the company's capabilities.

- Then the team worked together to create a Functional Construct that represents how the work of the company needs to be done. This was based on the three fundamental elements of functional work: enablement functions, execution functions, and supporting functions.

- We constructed Roles and Responsibilities Sheets to document what each functional team will do to get the work of the company done. As you may recall, a fundamental premise here was that if it's an important activity, it *must* land on one of these Roles and Responsibilities Sheets, but most importantly, it *must not* land on two or more sheets. This clarifies where accountability and responsibility lie for important work activities. This included the all-important determination of decision rights for each function, which is a fundamental aspect of ensuring alignment, the subject of this chapter.

- Finally, we established Tracking Sheets for each of the functions, listing the most important metrics (no more than ten) for measuring each function's success (based on the True North goals) for the fiscal period, balancing financial, operational, employee, and customer metrics.

With all this in place, put together and agreed upon by the operational leadership, or middle management, of the company, it is now time to cascade The Management System down into the company and ensure alignment across the entire organization. Alignment happens across two dimensions of the management construct. First is the vertical dimension, meaning up and down the organization. Second is a horizontal dimension, which is across the enablement and execution functions of the organization. Let's discuss both forms of alignment.

Vertical Alignment

Let's start with vertical. I refer to the direct reports of the CEO, or the senior management team, as level one of the organization. Level two would be those people who report to the level one executives, and level three would be the people who report to the level two executives. A fundamental key to the success of The Management System is to have as flat an organization as you can, with as few levels reporting directly to the CEO as possible. As you probably know, in the concept of a lean organization, you work to optimize each process. You want to reduce the number of steps required to get the work done, and you want to reduce the number of levels of the organization required to get the work done. You should always check your organization to ensure that it is operating as leanly as possible, because it is very easy in growth-oriented companies for this approach to break down.

As I said above, by this point we will have put Tracking Sheets in place for all the level one executives of the company, which is the functional leadership team. Again, these Tracking Sheets have the most important metrics (up to ten) that each function needs to deliver in the current operational year to give the overall organization the best chance to meet or exceed the True North objectives. One secret to achieving organizational alignment in the vertical dimension is to cascade the Tracking Sheet for each function down into the lower levels of that function.

To give a simplified example of this, let's talk about a sales organization that has a $10 million bookings target for the year. The executive in charge of the sales function would have a $10 million bookings objective on the sales function Tracking Sheet. Let's say that this sales executive has five sales managers as direct reports. To cascade the Tracking Sheet metrics down into level two, each of these sales executives would have a $2 million bookings target. Thus, these five sales managers each have their own objectives, but the combination of all five will then roll up to meet the $10 million objective on the level one manager's Tracking Sheet. This is an example of cascading metrics down through the organization. To take this example further, each of the five level two sales managers have four sales reps each. Each of the sales reps reporting to the level two sales manager would have a $500,000 bookings target. The result is that you have twenty level three sales reps with $500,000 bookings targets that roll up to five level two sales managers, each with a $2 million bookings target, and that would roll up to a level one sales executive who carries the entire $10 million bookings target for that function.

In this example, the $10 million in bookings is the revenue required from this function to achieve its part of the company's True North objective. To keep this example simple, I've not overassigned anyone on their bookings target. Thus, nineteen of the twenty salespeople could make their bookings target right on the mark, but if one did not, it would mean that the function did not make its bookings target, and because of the importance of bookings to revenue, it is highly likely that the company's overall revenue objective would not be achieved. The advantage of cascading Tracking Sheets down into the organization is that individuals understand exactly how critical their performance is to the overall successful performance of the organization. And because these metrics are expressed on Tracking Sheets that are updated and reviewed monthly, this approach makes it relatively easy for management to understand where there are execution challenges within the organization.

Horizontal Alignment

The second dimension of alignment is horizontal. Let's go back to the Functional Construct where we outlined how the work of the organization is done. We started with enablement functions, which enable the work of the organization to be performed. We followed that up with the execution functions, which actually perform the work, creating the value of the organization in the marketplace. And then we went into the supporting functions, such as financial and human resources, which have a relationship with both the enablement and execution functions to support their work activities.

Think about the enablement and execution functions as a horizontal workstream. Your work starts with strategy, then moves to building products and solutions, then moves into marketing and preparing the market for those solutions, and then moves into the execution functions that deliver those solutions. It all starts with an evaluation of a market and hopefully ends with a delighted customer. In this construct there is work that starts and is then handed off, and then further work is performed, and that is handed off, and so on. This creates dependencies and accountabilities among each of the functions.

As a part of the initial off-site, when we introduce The Management System to a new company, we challenge the teams to define these dependencies and accountabilities for each of the intersecting functions of the enablement and execution functions. We look at the work of a specific function and how that work must be handed off to the downstream function. Each function is accountable for achieving its work, and the downstream function depends on that work being done. Defining those handoffs and accomplishing alignment between those intersecting functions is a critical aspect of operational efficiency.

This graphic shows horizontal interdependencies:

Strategy	Solutions Management	Solutions Development	Marketing	Sales/Account Management	Solutions Delivery	Support
Set the strategy	Define the solution	Build the solution	Build demand for the solution	Acquire customers for the solution	Implement the solution for customers	Maintain the solution for customers

How Vertical and Horizontal Alignment Work Together

The combination of vertical and horizontal alignment drives the accelerated transformation of an organization. As a result of vertical alignment, every employee within a function understands their specific role and the metrics for which they are accountable. Their responsibilities are clear. As a result of horizontal alignment, the functions now understand their relationships with all the other functions, and this creates alignment across the entire organization. For an organization to be *good*, it must operate effectively within each function. But for an organization to be *great*, it must also work frictionlessly *across all enablement and execution functions*!

From the beginning of this book, I've talked about the transparency of The Management System. You have seen how we work with the management team to establish a Functional Construct of *how* work is done within a company. You have seen how the team reaches an agreement about *where* that work should be done and develops the Roles and Responsibilities Sheets to articulate the work. Then the team develops Tracking Sheets that allow them to target the most important metrics from each of the functions required to reach or exceed their True North goals. The only thing that doesn't change in The Management System is True North. Every other aspect can be adjusted based on the needs of the business. Any variable compensation plans a company has must be based on achievement of True North objectives for the entire company, not on the individual objectives of a person or function. This helps foster alignment, because everyone in the organization is working toward those goals and is helping one another achieve them.

All metrics are transparent to the entire organization as well. All the Tracking Sheet metrics from every function are available for anyone to see—as they must be, because you want everyone within the organization to understand how the work is being done. This fosters operational leverage to improve performance or capitalize on opportunities. You want to extract all the experience and expertise available within your organization, and that can only be achieved through an ever-increasing understanding of how the organization works, how it performs, and how it adjusts when challenges arise—as they always do.

If you have customers and employees, you are going to have challenges. Challenges aren't the issue. What's essential is *being aware* when challenges present themselves, and then having a way to quickly address those challenges by making the necessary modifications to either your metrics or how the work is being done. The transparency of the Tracking Sheets, which show how each function is performing against their key metrics, is critical to senior management and everyone else understanding how the company is performing operationally and financially. It also results in a deeper understanding across the company of the implications of decisions that are made and how they impact the performance of the business.

Let's review a simple example of how this works: If a sales department is highly effective in forecasting, then it will book business in a way that allows the delivery organization, which is dependent on those bookings, to staff at the right time and in the right numbers to deliver on that new business. The better an organization gets at performing its operational metrics, the better the organization is at anticipating the work required to deliver its products and/or services. With this ever-improving understanding of how the business works, downstream organizational managers gain confidence in their ability to make the right decisions. In The Management System, you always want decisions to be made as close to where the work is being done as possible. You don't want everything going up the organization and back down. This is the traditional decision-making process, and we want to break it down because it is highly inefficient. Tracking Sheets enable you to see all the decisions that are being made in the operation, upstream, downstream, and horizontally, allowing you to manage effectively in response to those decisions and creating a much more efficient and effective organization.

Jeanne Hecht, Executive Chair at Lexitas, saw the benefits of shifting metrics to create alignment between two functions at the QHP company she works with:

> We were looking into how marketing could best help sales with demand generation. We saw that marketing was doing an amazing job, but the sales pipeline wasn't growing. Looking at the metrics, we determined that the number one job in marketing, at that point in time, should be to help

sales grow their pipeline through marketing qualified leads. So we shifted a lot of the marketing metrics and stopped focusing on them because they weren't as important then (although they probably would be important in eighteen months or so). What the company really needed marketing to focus on was driving brand awareness and generating marketing qualified leads.

As soon as the marketing function shifted its focus, we started to see the fruits of their labor: more customer meetings, customer calls, RFPs received, and real sales opportunities. Instead of marketing just focusing 100 percent of their attention on glossy brochures and the website and so on, they shifted to putting 20 percent of their attention there and 80 percent on getting qualified leads. And that adjustment was a huge help to sales and therefore the whole company.

Patti McNamara, CFO of Catalyst Clinical Research, recognizes that metrics need to be dealt with honestly in order to align the company with what's *really* happening in the business:

You define what metrics are most important and then you track them. You have to talk about them every month. And if they pop up red, you have to have a deep discussion about them and present your conclusions honestly. For example, last month we had an issue with gross margin. We had a really good discussion in finance and worked with resourcing ops on what we were going to do differently. And then we presented it to the leadership team. This helped them understand why gross margin, and thus the financials, were slightly off that month, why the metrics were red—which is why we had to explain what was happening. We made sure that everybody had clarity on the actions required, so they could learn from what happened.

In companies without The Management System, I could see this issue being brushed under the rug. The CFO is embarrassed because the finance controls aren't perfect, so she doesn't want to talk about it to her leadership team. But with The Management System, when it's red, you don't have a choice; you have to come clean with everyone, which creates a much healthier business atmosphere.

A company that achieves both vertical and horizontal alignment has an exponentially greater chance of succeeding than an organization that neglects either or both.

How Alignment Helps

The relationship between enablement and execution functions is linear. The work of the organization starts with the first enablement function step and works its way through the last execution function. This linear relationship is the foundation for systemic operational efficiency and effectiveness. Each of the supporting functions has a relationship with each of the enablement and execution functions, but that relationship is not systemic—it's episodic. Here is an example of how that relationship works: As we invest in companies that are at a growth inflection point, additional hiring is typically required in execution functions. Let's say that in order to achieve the 25 percent revenue growth a company wants to achieve in a fiscal year, it has to increase bookings by 100 percent year over year. To achieve that, they must hire ten new sales executives. The human resources function would be responsible for the recruiting process associated with this group of new sales executives. So the sales function is dependent on the human resources function to source candidates for these ten new sales executives. Sales also wants to interview prequalified candidates who have gone through the human resources process, so they're depending on human resources to prequalify identified candidates.

But there's more to this example. If the fiscal year is a calendar year, then the company can't wait until December to hire ten new sales executives. People have to be hired with sufficient time to be trained and then develop enough opportunities in their particular territories, which will produce sufficient bookings to make the revenue goal. Therefore, there must be an understanding of the sales window within human resources. Not only do they have to source qualified candidates to fill the desired ten new sales executive roles, but they also have to do it within the timeframe that enables the company to achieve its True North revenue goal. So human resources has this episodic—but very important—relationship with sales during this hiring process and must act in a way that is aligned with sales goals and with the financial goals of the whole company. This is what alignment is all about—and why it's so important.

The best example I know of a leader achieving alignment with Tracking Sheets, cascading them down into a function to produce a transformative result, was achieved by Ben Clark when he was Vice President of Support at Misys Healthcare. When he joined Misys, the company's customer satisfaction scores were painfully low, due in large part to a lack of alignment within the customer support function. This is how he dealt with the situation:

> We had huge challenges in our support organization. Our Net Promoter Score, which measures customer satisfaction, was embarrassingly low—minus seventy, or something like that. This was a large organization, with about nine hundred people, made up of fifteen or twenty different support

departments. And everybody was doing their own thing, trying to fix their own issues their own way, measuring the things that they thought were important. There was really no standardization, which led to confusion and poor performance.

So we decided to move Tracking Sheets down to the individual level in the entire support organization. We decided with the people in the organization what the key metrics were that we had to measure—such as response time, resolution time, and so on—and then we were able to figure out what tactics would enable them to positively affect those measurements. Once they had that transparency, once they understood what would be measured, what needed to get done, people really responded. Within just six months, we were able to bring our Net Promoter Score up to a decent level and continue to improve on it over time.

Ben's leadership and deployment of Tracking Sheets throughout the support organization resulted in the company completely transforming its performance, which was a direct link to greater customer satisfaction with the solutions Misys was providing.

Nik Morton, President and COO of Catalyst Clinical Research, describes how important it was, once the company started growing rapidly, to push The Management System down to the next level. The following org chart shows the levels of an organization into which The Management System tools must be pushed down.

This was Nik Morton's experience with cascading the system down through his organization:

> To move The Management System to level two, we started a pilot process with one function before pushing it down into the entire organization. I picked one of the functions, one of the most complex parts of the business, and we broke down all the elements of their workflow, determined the roles and responsibilities for each of the departments within the function, and made sure accountabilities were clear. We developed a whole set of additional Tracking Sheets for this second level and instigated a monthly review meeting with the department heads to look at their part of the business and how it collaborated with its peers, how it fed the level one management system metrics.
>
> The process of defining The Management System at level two helped us clear up areas of ambiguity and get a stronger understanding of what each department within the function did and where their accountabilities lie. We took the level one metrics to a more granular level within level two, assigning measures of success for each of the departments.

Then we introduced the A3 process and root cause analysis and recovery planning, which allowed them to address some of the challenges they'd been facing in a very simple manner and get support from their peers and their management because of the transparency.

When we introduced this level two process to the rest of the business, we made it clear to middle management that we needed them to step up in order to achieve the next level of growth, that we would be holding them more accountable for discharging their responsibilities and delivering on their metrics, but we also made it clear that we wouldn't ask them for that without giving them the same kind of support that those at level one had gotten.

This approach was hugely successful at Catalyst, which grew at a record rate over the year following the introduction of the level two use of The Management System.

Sometimes a company requires a kind of "refresher off-site." This can be because the company has grown very fast organically or, even more so, if a new company is acquired. Sometimes it's just good to revisit what was established at the original off-site, to make sure it still applies and make any changes that might be necessary. QHP's Abby Decker describes how doing this can be useful:

> I think there is a lot of value in pulling the team together for three days a year to reset, realign, and have big, overarching conversations about where to go from where we are. We recently sat in on an off-site refresh for Catalyst, which has been operating under The Management System for several years. They decided to fly everyone in and start from the beginning by asking the question: Do we still agree with our

mission? What are our current strengths and weaknesses? Is our Functional Construct designed the right way? They were able to get realigned and feel prepared to kick off the year by just spending three days together. This can drive a lot of value for an organization—especially if they have employees around the world.

In my experience, companies encounter challenges with employee engagement and execution performance as a direct result of their employees not being aware of strategy, not understanding how the company operates overall, and not being clear about where they fit in, how their performance in a specific job is critical to the company's success. Clarifying those things for every employee in the organization is essential to the successful execution of the work required for a company to be successful.

For us at QHP, as private equity investors, we typically need to work with growth-oriented companies, so it is critical that we get the kind of alignment I'm talking about in this chapter early in our investment period. With a three- to seven-year window for value creation to produce a targeted return on the capital of our limited partners, we can't afford to waste a moment once the investment is made. Using The Management System, including cascading Tracking Sheets down through the organization, clarifies the work, responsibilities, and specific objectives that matter for every individual within the organization.

In my mind, there is nothing more important than every person in the organization having an understanding of where the company is going, where they fit within the organization, what they are accountable for, what decision rights they enjoy, and the specific metrics that they are responsible for meeting—metrics that will be transparently articulated throughout the organization to ensure the successful execution of everyone's work. Getting the right people into the right jobs is the most important thing that a manager can do at any level. I've always said that the job is easy when you have good people, but it is a challenge when you don't. The key to getting good people is providing clarity about the things I just described, enabling you to promote a culture of commitment and success, which attracts the best talent.

As one would expect when working with a company that is coming out of their early development stage into a growth stage, The Management System represents a significant change in how the work of the organization is being done. This change affects everyone in the organization, but it affects the CEO and senior leadership the most, because up until this point they have pretty much been making every significant decision. That approach to management, as natural as it is for start-ups, is one of the constraints to growth. The Management System facilitates the breaking down of that constraint and unleashes the full potential of every individual in the organization.

Successfully implementing The Management System requires the complete commitment of the CEO/founder and senior management team. As a part of our investment process at QHP, we always make sure we have this buy-in before closing a transaction. It is critical that they understand what The Management System will do, both the extensive benefits that it can produce for a company in its growth phase and the significant changes it requires in how the company operates. What the company does in the present is not what is required for it to realize its full potential in the future.

During the one-week off-site we conduct with each company we partner with, in which we begin to implement The Management System, it is sometimes very difficult for people to fully commit to this change. But during that off-site, which involves the entire senior management team, including the CEO/founder, *everybody has an equal vote*. Ultimately, this produces total buy-in by those in attendance because they are the ones shaping this new system to fit the way they do business. We don't dictate the particulars; we just provide the management framework for them to fill in according to the work they need and want to get done in order to grow. This approach is the secret to breaking down the barriers to change and creating an aligned management team, all of whom are working together for the achievement of the True North goals that they set for themselves in partnership with QHP.

7

WHEN THINGS DON'T GO ACCORDING TO PLAN

I n the fall of 2019, our portfolio companies were going through the exercise of locking down their operational plan for the fiscal year 2020. They were assessing their capabilities and the competitive landscape, working on plans to ensure they could execute against their growth opportunities, and in many cases preparing for inorganic transactions that needed to be integrated and operationalized. The Management System had provided a great format and foundation for this important work. The results of this work were modifications to roles and responsibilities for each function and the establishment of priority tracking metrics to measure success and performance against the operational plan, the True North goals. January 2020 arrived, and the teams within each company got to work.

Then, in the spring, COVID-19 hit. Everyone's world changed immediately, and for many companies, that change was definitely for the worse. There are countless stories of companies that were victimized by COVID-19 and did not survive. But there are stories about other companies (such as Chick-fil-A, which I discussed earlier in the book) that saw this dramatic change in the world as an opportunity and maintained their level of success due to the way they responded to change.

The point I'm making is that if you function in the world and have employees and customers, things are not always going to go according to plan! That's what good management is fundamentally all about: dealing successfully with change, with things not going according to plan. How do leaders and managers successfully deal with the never-ending set of challenges and opportunities that are presented to them on a daily basis? The Management System provides a foundation that management teams can use to evaluate on a factual basis the actions necessary to deal with any issue or challenge that arises and turn it into an opportunity.

No matter how good your plan is, things will never go exactly according to plan. For this reason, it is critically important that the fundamental elements of The Management System are in place and supported by the senior management team as a foundation for successful operational execution. I've talked about these foundational elements extensively in this book, but let's review them one more time:

- You have aligned your organization on strategy with the From-To Chart.

- You have put your Functional Construct into place, establishing the enablement, execution, and supporting functions.

- You have documented what happens in each function with up-to-date Roles and Responsibilities Sheets.

- Your Tracking Sheets are in place for each function and include the most important metrics that align with your True North goals.

If your company is like most companies, you'll have somewhere between ten and eighteen functions identified to support the work of your business. This means that you will have somewhere between 100 and 180 critical metrics to measure the successful operation of the business in your pursuit of True North. Each Tracking Sheet has targets for its metrics for each month of the year. If these metrics are critical to your achievement of your True North goals, then, naturally, if any metric is not on plan for the current month, you must have a process in place for getting that metric back on plan.

In the business world I "grew up" in, this typically meant that the executive responsible for a metric not being achieved would assess the issue and prepare a PowerPoint presentation, or some other document, to describe the situation. I have sat through countless PowerPoint presentations where executives, with their inherent biases and parochialisms, tried to justify why the problem was neither their fault nor the fault of their function. Those presentations typically did not address or identify an executable plan to get the metric back on target. So, at the end of the day, they were a complete waste of everyone's time, because they did not have a viable method for remediating the problem.

Business consultant Jeanne Hecht, who I've referenced previously in the book, describes how the A3 approach to dealing with problems changed the culture at Lexitas, a QHP portfolio company she works with:

When I first arrived, there was artificial harmony at Lexitas. It wasn't based on the kind of honesty and trust that allowed people to recognize when things were not going right and fix them. Finally, at one point, HR not only overspent on hiring salespeople but got the wrong people to boot. So the CEO finally challenged managers to be honest and open about uncovering problems, to use A3s effectively to delineate where the problems were, and to come up with solutions for them. The focus needs to be on the problem. It's not a criticism of the person if a metric is red, so they shouldn't have to be defensive and try to hide things. They should just write an honest A3 and work with the operating committee to find a solution.

In the business world that we live in today, if you are a growth company, you are limited in resources and limitless in opportunities to pursue. Time is the most crucial asset for you to manage. In the context of problem-solving or addressing challenges in the business, there are two elements that are crucial to managing your time. First is the quick identification of any issues, and second is the quick identification of a plan everyone agrees on that will remediate the issue.

Regarding the identification of issues, Tracking Sheets do a wonderful job of keeping you focused on the most important metrics and understanding whether those metrics are on target. The metric is either red or green: if it's green—on target—you keep on moving, and if it's red—not on target—you quickly develop and execute a plan to get it back on target. If you and your team have done a good job of identifying the top metrics and operationalizing them against the twelve months of the fiscal period, then you have the system you need to quickly identify when things are not going according to plan. It is when the latter happens that you employ The Management

System's last tool, a practical, flexible, and highly effective tool (if used correctly) that we call the A3.

What Is an A3?

It should be clear by now that a company in a period of accelerated growth must be able to manage business decisions effectively in the moment, and that includes problem-solving. The A3 enables you to do that. An A3 is a single sheet of paper on which the assessment of the problem is identified and the action plan for remediating the problem is laid out clearly and briefly. The fact that it is a single sheet of paper is important for a number of reasons. What I disliked so much about overly long PowerPoint presentations about problems was that I never knew when the presenters were going to get to the point. And when they did, the action plan was often just a variety of opinions about how to deal with the problem, contributed to by a variety of people. This is why the "solution" was rarely executed successfully; there just wasn't enough clarity. By putting everything on a single sheet of paper with prescribed categories of information required, you create a clear, common language for problem-solving.

This is important at every level of an organization. It doesn't matter if you're dealing with an issue at the CEO level or in the depths of the organization—everyone is looking at a common format for problem delineation and solving. There is no time wasted trying to tease out what the real problem is or coming up with an action plan. That is all laid out in the A3, which results in quick agreement about what the issue is and a robust discussion of the action plan required to remediate it. This leverages all the experience and expertise of the operating committee (or in whichever group you're using the A3), ensuring that the best action plan is put in place to solve the problem.

There are three types of A3s: Remedial, Project, and Strategy. Remedial is by far the most often used and is the basis for all three, so I will focus on it first and at greater length than the other two.

The elements of an A3, which establish that common language for problem-solving that I just referenced, are as follows:

- The left-hand side of the page presents the problem to be solved and includes the following items:

- The metric that is red and an identification of the current gap in the plan

- Relevant background information important to the performance issue that has led to the problem

- The root cause of the problem—the most important element that will be used to determine and reach agreement on an action plan

- The right-hand side of the page presents the action plan to remediate the problem and contains the following items:

- Description of the specific actions that will be taken, who will be responsible for taking them, and the date by which those actions should be taken

- Identification of the resources required to execute the action plan that are not in the direct control of the owner of the metric being remediated

The A3 provides a common format and a common language that allows the effective use of your talent pool when problem-solving. When you look at the top left of the A3, it is clear what metric you are focusing on and the current gap in your performance against plan. The discussion of the background that follows provides context for how your performance gap has developed. Then comes the most important element: root cause. If you do not understand the root cause of the problem that is creating the performance gap, then your action plan will have little chance of success.

There is an effective technique for determining the root cause of a problem that is called "the five whys." The concept here is to ask why the performance gap has happened, come up with a cause, and then ask why that cause happened. Then you dig down to find out why *that* cause happened. You need to be brutally honest about finding each cause. You repeat this process at least five times, continually digging deeper into each cause until you're certain you've really gotten down to the *root cause* of the problem. It's important to push this process all the way, to not settle for a cause that does not get to the root of the problem; otherwise, you will not be able to solve that problem.

When I have management teams off-site for the implementation of The Management System and we discuss the five whys, I ask them to go home and try it with their spouse, children, family, or friends when they are trying to get to the root of a problem. And they find that the technique really works! The point is that you *must* understand the *fundamental* cause for the performance gap if you're going to put together an effective action plan to remediate it.

My fellow QHP Partner Michael Sorenson tells a great story about using the five whys on an A3 to discern the cause of delivery problems at a drug company, where customers were receiving incomplete and delayed shipments. By continuing to ask, "Why is this happening?" over and over again about their approach to shipping, they got it all the way down to the level of the guy in charge of loading the pallets in the warehouse and discovered that *he* was the one deciding which shipments went on which truck pallets. He was simply trying to fill up pallets for shipments without any knowledge of which shipments were most important or needed to be kept together! So the process can lead to some surprising root causes.

Now let's move to the right side of the A3, where you focus your energy on putting together an action plan that addresses the root cause and allows you to quickly close your performance gap. You're identifying the actions required and the resources needed across the organization to rectify a metric, a metric that you consider critical to achieving your True North objectives for the year. So it's important! Using the A3 allows you to eliminate time-wasting PowerPoint presentations and removes politics, parochialism, and biases from the process of solving a problem—because, as Jeanne Hecht noted, the focus is on the problem, not the people.

As an executive, this approach also allows you to see very quickly who on your team can really solve problems and successfully execute a problem-solving plan versus those who are just good at talking about problems, not at solving them. Because your company is in a period of accelerated transformation, you can't afford to waste time. Being able to quickly identify issues and put together a plan to remediate them is a huge differentiator for companies trying to grow quickly.

On the surface, this single sheet of paper approach to highlighting and remediating problems sounds easy. The format is all laid out, and you simply have to fill it in. But most companies find it to be more challenging than they initially think it will be. An A3 requires that you *really know your business*. And it's not about the number of words that you can jam onto a single page. It's about ensuring that the left side of the page properly documents the issue and the right side properly documents the plan to remediate—and all this *should be stated in as few words as necessary for clarity*.

The benefit to doing this thoughtfully is that, as you are executing against your plan, you now have a document that everyone is using as a collaboration tool as they take the actions needed to remediate the issue. There is no confusion about the action plan. There is no confusion about who owns it. And because you're dealing with a metric that is objective, there is no confusion about whether, in the end, you are being successful with your plan to remediate. The A3 document is a collaboration tool. You collaborate to identify the problem effectively; you collaborate to put the best plan in place to remediate; and then you collaborate to execute the remediation plan. And you don't stop until the metric has returned to green. Once you've accomplished that, you declare victory, put the A3 in a drawer, and get back to work.

Managing Your A3s Effectively

Your company has put together its operational plan and articulated that plan through metrics on Tracking Sheets. These are metrics that the company is looking to grow into, achieve through operational improvements, or aggressively pursue. Being in a period of accelerated growth means that all your metrics will *not* be green all the time. In fact, if you have a function within your company that is setting metrics that are layups—and will therefore always be green—that function and its leader are not committed to what is required to perform in a period of accelerated growth. In any given month, as you're reviewing the metrics across all your functions, you may have forty or fifty metrics that are red and require A3s. This is no reason to panic! This is the way the system is supposed to work. I'd like to share a couple of things about managing your A3s.

For every metric on a Tracking Sheet that is red—not on plan— the functional owner of that Tracking Sheet needs to prepare a Remedial A3. The writing of the A3 must start as soon as a manager realizes that a metric is not on plan—not at the last minute before the operating committee meeting. At the operating committee meeting, for every metric that is red, the functional executive must present an A3 that describes how that metric is going to return to green.

But not all A3s have the same importance. Context matters. For example, if we miss a $10 million bookings target in the month of March by a dollar, the metric is still red, but it's an insignificant red. If sales is forecasting across the next three months that they're going to make their bookings target, then a dollar miss in the month of March does not require a review with the senior management team. However, if sales missed a $10 million bookings target for the month of March by a dollar and the forecast for the next three months is a more significant miss month after month, then we do need an A3 and most likely a review of the plan to remediate with the senior management team.

All red metrics require an A3; however, the most important ones are the ones that should be reviewed monthly with the senior management team to ensure that the best possible plan of action is being put in place and is fully resourced. Again, these are the most important metrics on your journey to True North, and everyone's variable comp is determined based on performance against True North. The senior management team will want to ensure that each important metric is being taken seriously, and the owners of the A3s should be working with their teams to execute the action plan to bring their metrics back to green.

For the operating committee meeting, after reviewing the Tracking Sheets, the committee should determine the A3s for which a review and discussion with the senior management team is appropriate. Depending on the significance of the metrics involved, this could result in just a few or many A3s being reviewed. As I've said, reviewing these A3s with the senior management team ensures that the right root cause has been identified and the best possible action plan is in place. Equally important is the operating committee discussion about how to resource these action plans, because there are always consequences and trade-offs when applying resources to the most important issues of the day.

Discussing A3s in the operating committee meeting means that the issue will be understood by everyone on the senior management team, the people who have the power to allocate the resources required to execute an action plan. This also allows the senior management team to clearly articulate to their respective functions the reasons for decisions made. And it ensures that messaging is consistent throughout the organization—and aligned messaging is an important aspect of The Management System's effectiveness. You're trying to maximize the utilization of your limited resources and ensure that everyone understands where the challenges are in the business and how resources are being allocated to address those challenges. That alignment ensures focus by the entire organization, and that focus results in consistent, successful execution against the most important metrics for achieving True North objectives.

Two Other Types of A3s

It may have occurred to you while reading the description of a Remedial A3 that the form might be useful in situations other than dealing with off-target metrics, and you're right. There are two additional types of A3s that are useful in other situations: Project A3s and Strategy A3s.

PROJECT A3

When your organization is inducing change that affects multiple functions of your organization, I recommend using Project A3s as a way of justifying the project. This ensures that a project has a plan that delivers on the objective and communicates progress against that plan over time. This is usually a project targeted toward executing an initiative that is cross-functional, where two or more functions within the company are working together on the project. Examples of a project that could benefit from the use of an A3 are the implementation of a CRM or ERP system, the development of a new website, or the implementation of a new go-to-market approach. As the first element on the left-hand side of the page, the Project A3 would have—instead of a metric—the objectives that the organization is looking to achieve as a result of the implementation of the project. The right-hand side of the page would articulate the project plan, including owners of project actions and dates for achieving different milestones.

STRATEGY A3

The process of evaluating and executing a new strategy is another instance where an A3 can be useful. This is usually a larger strategic initiative, which typically incorporates a perspective beyond the current operational or fiscal year, looking at something larger and more long term—an acquisition, for example. The left side of the A3 would include a high-level articulation of the objective of the strategy, with background about why it is being considered and what the strategy would address in the market. The left side would articulate the action plan to execute the strategy, with responsibilities and delivery dates for taking the actions. This A3 is useful for vetting a strategy with the operating committee and soliciting approval and support for it.

As with Remedial A3s, the benefit of this approach for project and strategy efforts is the common format and common language it establishes, which enables everyone involved to buy in, focus on the most important and most appropriate elements of the project or strategy, and contribute to developing the most robust plan for achieving the project's or strategy's objectives.

One Special Kind of A3: The Burning Platform

There is one type of A3 that is so important we've given it its own name: the Burning Platform A3. A Burning Platform A3 can be a Remedial, Project, or Strategy A3, but it concerns a metric so critical that achieving it affects the entire organization and its ability to achieve True North. In the early days of The Management System, and in the early days of my experience as a CEO, the situations that I faced were more transformationally oriented, because the companies were significantly challenged in their operational performance or performance against competitors in their markets. As a result, some significant metrics—for example, revenue or EBITDA or cost initiatives—critical to the success of the company were not only from an operational perspective but from a strategic perspective. Keeping these metrics green was critical to staying on plan and to the transformation of the organization as a whole, so they affected everyone in the company. When any of those numbers were off, a Burning Platform A3 was assigned to me, the CEO, who took ownership of the problem. So a Burning Platform A3 is one for which the metric is so critical to the whole organization and to successfully reaching True North that the CEO personally takes over the responsibility for getting that metric back on plan.

Creative Uses of A3s

As I said earlier, the A3 is a highly flexible tool, and it has been used by the companies we work with in many creative ways. Here are some examples that you might imitate and that might inspire you to find your own creative uses for A3s.

IMPROVING CUSTOMER SATISFACTION

Mike Raymer, currently the CEO of Pro-ficiency, describes how using an A3 uncovered the root cause of a significant customer satisfaction problem when he was at MedFusion:

> When we first looked at the metrics, it seemed like the support organization was doing a terrible job of managing customers. Why? Because the customer response ratings were low, and the number of interactions support was having with customers was much higher than it should have been. But when we wrote up an A3 and continued to ask why, we were able to trace the problem back primarily to the fact that our core software was too buggy and therefore didn't work very well. The A3 illuminated that.

> So we assigned a group of our development organization to burn down the bug count. It was a nine- to twelve-month plan with metrics that called for significant bug reduction—and it worked. We were able to drive down the bug count substantially, which, not surprisingly, reduced the number of support calls dramatically and significantly improved customer satisfaction.

> So the original Tracking Sheet metrics pointed out the customer problem, and then the A3 exploration got down to

the root cause of the problem—which was *not* our support organization, but the product they were trying to support. That enabled us to focus on the work that *really* needed to be done to correct the problem.

Faisal Mushtaq was the head of R&D at Misys when The Management System was introduced, and he was quickly able to see the value of the A3 in helping solve a customer satisfaction issue:

> We had a significant customer satisfaction problem because our software was not supporting smooth implementation on an important interface. It was a problem that we needed to resolve quickly, and I knew it could potentially take months and months to resolve, so I decided to have somebody document the problem on an A3.
>
> Due to the clarity of the A3 structure, this person was able to ask the right questions, talk to the right people, populate the A3 with the essential information about the issue, and present a plan on how to resolve it. This was so much more effective than just talking to people and putting together a PowerPoint presentation. With the A3 in hand, we were able to talk through the issues and realize that the problem really came down to priorities. Since everyone had a different set of goals, we went through the A3. This sensitized everybody to the severity of the customer issue and taught them why they should care. And once we got to the point where we all agreed that solving this problem was a priority, everyone was on board for solving it together. The A3 was fundamental to getting to that point of common understanding.

SOLVING A TURNOVER PROBLEM

Jeanne Hecht, who talked previously about the overall value of A3s, also has a good story about how Lexitas employed an A3 to deal with a turnover problem:

> Lexitas did not have a very professional culture when we started working with them. Because of this, people who came in from really established companies didn't survive very long. They wanted processes and systems and metrics, and there was none of that. So we got into a discussion about: What is our mission, our vision, our values, our way of working? What do we want the culture to be here?
>
> We went back to what we'd written about culture originally and thought about how it needed to evolve. We put together an A3 that focused on all the key elements of culture. That led us to spending a lot of time talking with employees across the organization, doing focus groups, and making sure that our mission, vision, and values resonated with people—that how the company was run and how people behaved would attract and retain good employees.
>
> This process was highly successful. Lexitas's turnover rate is tiny now, something like 4 percent, and we haven't lost any critical hires. This is unheard of.

IMPROVING PRODUCTION EFFICIENCY

Ajay Damani, CEO of CoreRx, and his team uncovered inefficiencies in their custom drug production that saved the company from a dramatically expensive approach to solving the problem:

We were not satisfied with our rate of production, and the management team at the time was recommending that we move from a two-shift model to a three-shift model. There was a lot of discussion around this topic because it was an expensive move. And it turned out, the manufacturing leadership at the time didn't have the right level of understanding or information to help the management team understand how to think through this type of decision.

This is a perfect example of how The Management System brought discipline, rigor, and accountability to the process. We had figured out what key production metrics drove the operation. We had developed metrics around efficiency, turnaround time, productivity, and so on. And we found that we were not coming close to our KPIs in these areas. Laying out the problem like this started to raise questions around whether we were focusing on the right problem, meaning going from two shifts to three shifts, because it didn't seem like our head count and cost base was even close to the point where we should contemplate an additional shift.

Ultimately, we decided that the problem was poor leadership in manufacturing. And we were fortunate enough to find someone in-house with stellar drug production leadership experience. With this new leader in place, we not only didn't have to add a new shift, but during his first year we reduced head count by fifteen and achieved a record level of productivity, and ultimately revenues, in the manufacturing part of the business. This all came out of getting down to the real problem using The Management System tools.

DEMONSTRATING RESOLVE TO INVESTORS

My QHP colleague Karol Jarzabek used to work for Azurity, one of our portfolio companies. He took on the task there of trying to reinvigorate a generic drug division that was just limping along. He came to QHP for additional funding and used A3s as part of his presentation. Here's how he tells the story:

> One thing I like about A3s, if they're done well, is that they substantiate someone's resolve to improve things. We were at a point with the generics division at Azurity that there was pressure to sell it because it wasn't performing well for us. But I saw real potential there—and, at the very least, I knew we had to improve the business in order to make it attractive to potential buyers. I met with the QHP Partners and presented my case for additional investment in the division.
>
> All the work we were doing to improve the business—and it was substantial—was reflected in the A3s we showed there. The Tracking Sheets showed the key metrics we were measuring, and the A3s showed exactly what we were doing to improve those metrics. You could see the profile of the business and get a clear sense of where it was going. And it was clear that the division had significant unrealized potential. I got the green light, QHP invested further, and by the end of the year, not only did we hit our goals, but we also helped Azurity's bottom line—and Azurity ultimately retained the division, instead of selling it, because it was so profitable.

To reiterate what I said at the beginning of this chapter, no plan can be executed flawlessly, and success or failure depends on how you react when things don't go according to plan. The Management System is very good at both making you aware of problems as soon as they arise, with Tracking Sheets, and providing a structure for dealing with those problems, using A3s. Using the A3 format and driving this discipline into the entirety of the organization enables everyone to become a problem solver. Famed inventor Thomas Edison once said, "I have not failed. I've just found ten thousand ways that won't work." The Management System does a great job of helping you find the ways that *do* work.

Adjusting Priorities and Pursuing Opportunities

In the framework of The Management System, the only things that cannot be changed for any given year are the True North objectives. As you go through a year where you're performing against True North, the management team will consistently assess the performance of the team, the traction in the marketplace, the macro and competitive pressures and threats, and all the fundamental dynamics of trying to manage a business. The only meeting required within The Management System framework is the monthly operating committee meeting, where every functional leader reviews their Tracking Sheet and the committee reviews the prioritized A3s.

The beauty of these meetings and this framework is that you're able to adjust the priorities of the team, the functions of the company, based on the dynamics of the marketplace. I've already shared the story of one of our portfolio companies, which had consistently outperformed their bookings metrics quarter after quarter, when suddenly they were short on their revenue projections. This was the data that appeared on the Tracking Sheet. One of their strategies, and one of the compelling aspects for our investment in the business, was their potential for selling *bigger* projects. It turned out that they were, in fact, booking bigger contracts, but that revenue was realized over a forty-eight-month period, therefore producing less revenue within the current fiscal year than the projected revenue from the twenty-four-month project. What was beautiful about this conversation was that, once everyone understood what the facts were, the only question was how many more bookings they needed to achieve their revenue objective. That calculation was made, and the Tracking Sheet was changed to reflect the change in goal. This was all done in about a fifteen-minute period of time!

Because these operating committee meetings look at performance against all the Tracking Sheet metrics, every executive learns about how the business performs and how the functions need to work together to execute the business. Sitting in that room as a function owner on a month-to-month basis, being presented performance against the Tracking Sheet by every other functional leader, enables you to have a true senior management view about the priorities of the business and allocating resources. You get commitment from your management team and enhance their capabilities this way. You accelerate decision-making, which makes your company nimbler. All of this enhances the company's opportunity to achieve its True North goals and realize its full potential.

As you sit through the monthly operating committee meeting and review your company's performance against all the metrics that are captured on the Tracking Sheet, opportunities as well as problems will emerge. The question is: How do you act on those opportunities? For example, you're losing to a competitor because they have a certain capability that you don't have. How do you determine whether you should invest in that capability or not? Or you could learn that you're winning in a market segment that you did not believe you could win. Then the question becomes: How do we more vigorously pursue that segment? The Management System provides a framework to deal with these opportunities.

In the operating committee meeting, the review of Tracking Sheets should expose these opportunities. And because of the development of the Functional Construct, you should now have a strategic function that can deal with the evaluation of these opportunities. The enablement functions evaluate strategies and capabilities, develop a business case for the investments required to successfully execute against opportunities, and determine what the return on those investments should be. The enablement functions deal with the road map execution that comes from the From-To Chart and deal with how you prioritize opportunities that present themselves each year. They evaluate the trade-offs that are required and the investments that are needed, and they put a plan in place that articulates how the rest of the organization would have to change to execute against a given opportunity. Cross-functional interaction via operating committee meetings allows the engagement of all the other functions in the enablement function's business planning process, which facilitates buy-in and full support of any plan that is approved.

This framework allows a company to rapidly evaluate opportunities and its ability to pursue them. The only useful answers about new opportunities are yes and no. The Management System facilitates quick evaluation and decision-making about new opportunities and the communication of the decision to pursue an opportunity throughout the organization—once again keeping the organization aligned and focused on the most important work that needs to be done. Being able to evaluate new opportunities and pursue them swiftly facilitates the acceleration and transformation of the company.

In addition to the monthly operating committee meetings, we ask our portfolio companies to facilitate a mini off-site in the November/December timeframe to evaluate their performance over the past year and operationalize their plan for the following year. With the initial implementation of The Management System, there is a lot of discussion and debate as those involved decide how to complete the initial work. But after a company has operated in The Management System framework for a year, it has a good understanding of how to operate within the system and assess what can be done to improve processes. Obviously, the financial expectations of the company that's in a growth mode will result in True North objectives that are greater than the preceding year.

During this mini off-site, they assess every element of The Management System, starting with an evaluation of their strategy and how much progress they've made against their five-year plan. They reassess the SWOT Analysis to also see how much progress they've made throughout the year. They check themselves against their values to ensure that the management team is leading the company in the right direction so that everyone is responding with the behaviors necessary to develop the culture of success. They make sure that the Functional Construct still reflects how the work of the company should be done and review all the Roles and Responsibilities Sheets to ensure that the work is being done in the right place. They revalidate their resourcing to ensure that they have the right talent in all the functions and, finally, they populate their Tracking Sheets with the metrics necessary for each function to contribute to the True North objectives. The Management System is a practice, and the organization continues to learn about itself and how it executes against its objectives. As a result, the company gets better and better and better, year after year after year. This enables not only the acceleration of the company's transformation but the acceleration of its growth and enhances the probability of it realizing its full potential.

And the goal is *always* to make sure that your company is realizing its full potential. The way that is achieved is by developing a new rhythm for your business, and in the next chapter I'll show how each of The Management System tools I've described plays a role in that new business rhythm.

8

YOUR NEW BUSINESS RHYTHM

The Management System is both operationally and financially focused. It is built on the premise that we are tracking the metrics that are most important from each of the functions of your organization in order to meet or exceed your True North objectives for the year. Therefore, you need a mechanism that enables you to manage effectively within the construct of this system. The senior management team needs to come together regularly to review the performance of the company against Tracking Sheet metrics, make the adjustments required to deal with areas that are challenged, and gear up performance for new opportunities that present themselves. This approach establishes a new business rhythm for your company, a rhythm that maintains focus across the organization and ensures that the important things get done, day to day, month to month, year to year. As I've said before, the purpose of The Management System is to ensure that the right work is being done. You must ensure that your limited resources are being directed toward efforts that have the maximum impact on your performance as you march toward your True North goals.

Joanna Williams, COO of Lexitas Pharma Services, describes how The Management System changed the way things were handled in a founder-led company that needed to transform itself in order to grow:

> In a founder-led company like ours, each person would be wearing a lot of different hats, and there was no clear delineation of "lanes," of roles and responsibilities. The approach was, whatever job needs to be done, somebody will do it. So things started to get all tangled up. And we didn't have a lot of metrics based on real data, so we couldn't make decisions with very much discipline. We did a lot of things based on our gut feelings, without clear targets and goals. We just didn't manage the business the way a business has to be managed to grow.

> When we introduced The Management System, we were able to detangle all the functions of the business, make a clear delineation of roles and responsibilities and accountabilities, and establish which metrics were important in the business. It forced us to see clearly what each function needed to do to get the important work done. We walked out of the off-site that introduced The Management System with a very clear set of responsibilities, accountabilities, and tracking measures that would be based on collecting real data. It was a whole new rhythm for our business.

In working with our portfolio companies, we have found that the best practice is to have a monthly operating committee meeting. That is what I called this meeting when I was CEO, and it's what I recommended our portfolio companies call it. Once a month, all the functional leaders of the company come together to review the performance of the company end to end, across all the functions. As you recall from the Tracking Sheet chapter, the team has determined the most important metrics per function across a balanced scorecard, meaning that each function has metrics that are, ideally, financially oriented, operationally oriented, customer oriented, and employee oriented. These metrics have been chosen because they represent the most important metrics for that function to perform against in the pursuit of the True North goals. As you operationalize your plan for the year, each month has a target for each objective. And for the structure of The Management System to hold, these metrics and the monthly targets must represent your operational plan on a monthly basis for the year on your journey to True North. The operating committee meeting is the one meeting a month where all the leadership comes together to review the Tracking Sheets and report on performance across all the metrics on those sheets.

But bear in mind that just *introducing* The Management System is no guarantee that it will be used *correctly* to change the rhythm of the business and put it on a path to greater efficiency and transparency. Phillip Shilling, Vice President of Business Operations for Azurity Pharmaceuticals, one of our portfolio companies, was brought in to get The Management System there back on track when it was not being used as it was meant to be:

> Azurity had not been disciplined about using The Management System. The organization would execute projects, but the project execution would not adhere to any kind of

rhythm. The organization didn't understand many of the key principles about project execution within The Management System, so projects were pursued without an organizational approach. Functions were operating in silos, as they always had.

This lack of discipline led to deliverables that did not meet the needs of the organization. My challenge was to convince each function to not just deliver on projects, but to deliver in a way that adhered to the metrics and goals of The Management System approach. Changing the functions' working mindset proved to be a challenge. When people are conducting their work in a certain manner, day in and day out, it becomes second nature, so it can be difficult to introduce a new way of working. I had to hammer away about the new approach, and I met some resistance, but once we enforced the discipline of The Management System, the teams came around.

The Management System enabled real transparency and made project management much more streamlined and efficient—which became evident to everyone after we achieved our refresh of the system and started using it as it was designed to be used.

Until The Management System is fully operational, establishing a new and more effective rhythm for your business, you cannot achieve the benefits of the system.

Structure of Monthly Operating Committee Meetings

Your monthly operating committee meetings need to have a consistent, workable structure and a clear agenda. Over the years, QHP has developed an agenda that we think is effective, and I'd like to share each part of that agenda with you.

CEO KICKOFF

This is a five- to ten-minute introduction delivered by the CEO, who should comment on the state of the company as you come into each monthly review. The commentary should highlight both the opportunities that are emerging for the business and the challenges that the business must overcome in order to succeed and grow. The kickoff is important for setting the tone for each individual operating committee meeting.

TRACKING SHEET REVIEW

The best practice here is to proceed in the linear fashion of the business, starting with the Tracking Sheets for enablement functions, then moving on to the execution functions and finally the supporting functions. This session should last one and a half to three hours maximum. Each functional leader should take five to ten minutes to review their Tracking Sheet and comment on the state of their function. This is an opportunity for functional leaders to demonstrate their knowledge of their function and their understanding of how the business works in relation to that function. This is not the time to do a deep dive into something that is not going according to plan. That is the purpose of A3 reviews. This is the moment for the functional leader to articulate opportunities both within their function and in the business as a whole and to also articulate the challenges their function is facing as they perform against their top ten metrics.

There are many benefits to reviewing Tracking Sheets on a monthly basis. Here are some of those benefits:

- **Time saving**: These reviews should eliminate the need for all kinds of ad hoc meetings that lack purpose or intentionality, which often occur within an organization. *This liberates each functional team to spend the month between reviews working on the business, not working on reporting on the business.* This is valuable because it frees up significant time and eliminates unnecessary meetings—for the CEO and everyone else.

- **Deeper understanding of the business**: Having the functional leaders in a room for the reports on *all* Tracking Sheets creates an opportunity for a deeper understanding across the entire management team about how the business works. In most companies that are going through their early growth stages, the understanding of the business rests with the founder or owner or CEO and a small number of people on the management team. The Functional Construct of The Management System and the establishment of Tracking Sheet reviews provide an opportunity for every functional leader to see how the company is performing across the board against the top metrics of *every* function in the company. Functional leaders continually enhance their understanding of the operational and financial levers of the business and the criticality of each metric for the journey to True North. This deeper understanding of how their function works in the context of the whole organization allows for better decision-making— both during the operating committee meeting and outside of operating committee meetings. *I cannot overstate how important and valuable scaling your business is to having all functional leaders engaged in this review and seeing how the entire business works.* I've seen long-tenured employees who were astonished by what they learned about the company after just one operational meeting.

- **Decision-making**: Important decisions about changes to priorities and about adjusting the work required to exceed True North goals are all made in these meetings. The beautiful thing here is that everyone understands *why* these decisions are being made and the *implications* of these decisions across functions. This creates alignment across the senior leadership team so that coming out of the operating committee meeting, no one is confused as to what the tasks and priorities are going forward.

- **Transparency**: *All* the most important metrics of the business are reported on in the operating committee meeting. Therefore, every member of the senior management team sees all aspects of the business—it is completely transparent to them. Clearly, there is a risk when this information is shared across the entire senior management team, but the benefits *significantly* outweigh the risks. This transparency contributes to the elimination of politics and parochialism, which are cancers in any organization and particularly harmful to companies trying to transform and grow.

- **Ability to adjust**: With any change of priorities going forward as a result of decisions made within the operating committee meeting, appropriate adjustments are made on the Tracking

Sheets. This provides clarity about the work that's required going forward.

- **Professional development**: As a result of senior leaders seeing the entirety of the metrics of the company on a monthly basis and having exposure to the discussions and debates that lead to decisions about adjustments required, a great deal of management development occurs. I honestly believe that sitting in on a year of operating committee meetings is equivalent to achieving an MBA! There is no better business training for the development of a senior executive than to be engaged in the discussions that occur within the operating committee meetings. There have been several members of management teams we've worked with who have gone on to be very successful CEOs. They could do this because they had experience across the totality of the functions of the company they came from. They achieved a deep and rich understanding about the work and priorities of the enablement, execution, and supporting functions. They understood how a company works across the board as well as the implications of decisions across all functions—not just the area in which they "grew up" in their professional career. Having this deep and broad understanding of the performance requirements across all functions absolutely enhances the skill set of managers. The Management System's operating committee meetings are a great primer for the development of senior executives and future CEOs.

REMEDIATION OF RED METRICS

The last agenda item is the remediation of metrics that are not going according to plan, the metrics that are red on the Tracking Sheets. I always say that if you've got employees and customers, things are *not* going to go according to plan. That is just the nature of business. As you look at the totality of the metrics that are being reviewed at the operating committee meeting, you may find you have as many as 120 to 160 most important metrics. And if a metric is critical on the path to meeting or exceeding True North goals, and has therefore landed on a Tracking Sheet, and if that metric is not on target, the functional leader must be prepared to present a plan to get that metric back to green at the operating committee meeting. This is done in the A3 format I discussed previously. The last part of your operating committee meeting needs to focus on the review of the most important A3s, the ones that warrant the attention of the entire senior management team.

Length of Operating Committee Meetings

The length of and division of time allotted for operating committee meetings is flexible. Here are three approaches that have worked for our partner companies.

FULL-DAY APPROACH

A full day, where you start in the morning with the CEO comments, then move to Tracking Sheets, finishing the remainder of the day with a review of the most urgent A3s.

TWO-FULL-DAYS APPROACH

Two individual day sessions, where you break down the Tracking Sheet and A3 reviews into two entirely separate sessions. The first day has the CEO commentary and reviews of all Tracking Sheets. Then the group chooses the A3s that they want to review in depth, and those reviews happen the next day. This approach results in a strong focus on the A3 reviews.

FULL-DAY-OVER-TWO-DAYS APPROACH

My personal preference is to start at noon on the first day of a two-day operations committee meeting. The team flies in that morning and gathers for lunch. The afternoon session begins with the CEO comments and the Tracking Sheet reviews. Depending on the condition of the company, you can move into A3 reviews that afternoon and continue into the evening, or you can have a senior management team dinner, where you talk about the status of the business. (One company I worked with was conveniently located near a great restaurant with a circular table in a private room. This table was big enough for the entire senior management team to gather around, and we found it to be a wonderful way for us to reconnect and talk as a group about the company, its performance, and the opportunities moving forward.)

The next morning, you continue with a review of your A3s and determine your strategic priorities going forward, ending at noon so the management team can travel in the afternoon and evening. An operating committee meeting can be quite grueling, so I like the idea of breaking it up into two sessions over two days (and having some relaxation as well), so you can maximize the attention and focus of all team members during the only meeting of the month.

Ultimately, your approach to operating committee meetings does not really matter—what matters is having them on a monthly basis—so you should pick the approach that best meets the needs of your team and company. What's important is that this is the one meeting each month during which metrics are reviewed, decisions are made, and alignment is achieved on the most important activities going over the next month and beyond. Once the metrics on the Tracking Sheets are established from the source data and calculations are completed and confirmed, the preparation for the operating committee meeting is very minimal. If I'm a functional leader, I have just ten metrics on my Tracking Sheet that have been computed and filled in a few days after the financial books of the business have closed for the month.

Speaking of metrics, functional leaders should never be surprised about whether a metric is on plan or not on plan as the Tracking Sheet is produced. If they know their function, they will know the minute that something is not going according to plan, whether it's Tracking Sheet time or not. It is at the point where they become aware of something not going according to plan that they should begin preparing an A3 to remediate any performance issue—the A3 that they will present at the operating committee meeting.

A Unifying Business Rhythm

As you may recall from when we developed the Functional Construct, business activities move linearly across the enablement functions and then across the execution functions, with supporting functions assisting both functions episodically. The enablement functions set the strategy and the business plans that are then put into action by the execution functions. So if you think about this in terms of the operating committee meeting and review of Tracking Sheets, the enablement functions are looking to see if the plans they put in place are being realized by the execution functions.

As I stated earlier, if you have employees and customers, things are *not* going to go according to plan at some point. The beauty of an operating committee review is that you get to see the metrics on the enablement functions that effectively represent the outcomes to be achieved by the execution functions. The combination of the enablement functions establishing the right priorities and plans and the execution functions performing according to those plans should result in the successful achievement of True North goals.

Seeing the review of all these metrics across enablement and execution functions enables tremendous learning and understanding about the performance of the company and the levers both financially and operationally within the company. But because things are not always going to go according to plan, everyone also gets to see what adjustments are required and what metrics need to be changed to ensure that the right work is being done as the company moves forward into the next month and the remainder of the year.

For me, the great thing about this approach is that the entire senior management team is involved in the discussion of a problem and tries to understand together what is going on. This can lead to big aha moments *for everyone.*

The Management System provides the operational framework that enables the management team to understand what is happening in the business and facilitate the required adjustments moving forward. Creating the Functional Construct to understand how the work of the company is done; creating the Roles and Responsibilities Sheets so that every function knows what their job is—and isn't; agreeing on the most important metrics that land on the Tracking Sheet for each function and are reviewed monthly in the operating committee meeting: all of this works together to create the best model I know for a company to accelerate their transformation and realize their full potential.

Week-to-Week Picture of the New Business Rhythm

In most companies, the financials for monthly reporting are completed somewhere between the seventh and fifteenth day after the end of the month. Once metrics on a Tracking Sheet are calculated and the source data they're drawn from is confirmed, it only takes each function a day or two to populate their Tracking Sheets. Ideally you want the operating committee meeting to be held as close as possible to the completion of the monthly financial books and the population of the Tracking Sheets. Therefore, operating committee meetings are typically held on the third week of the month and no later than early in the fourth week of the month. This produces a good cadence for the senior management team, executing the business for most of the month and then coming together to manage the business together.

This rhythm of business can be best articulated by looking at a month in four-week increments:

- **Week 1**: The team is executing the business as the financial team is assembling the monthly financial reports and working to close the preceding month's books.

- **Week 2**: The books are being closed and the Tracking Sheets are being populated with the preceding month's performance. If you're a functional leader, you will certainly know by the second week of the month whether you are on target or off target with your metrics. You should receive the prepared and populated Tracking Sheets from your direct reports during the second week of the month. The functional leader reviews the performance of the function against the metrics on its Tracking Sheet with the teams within the function. For red items on the Tracking Sheets, the team prepares the remediating A3 documents, which will be reviewed at the operating committee meeting—but, more importantly, they will start executing the activities needed to get the red metric back to green.

- **Week 3**: Functional leaders are preparing their commentary for the Tracking Sheet review at the operating committee meeting and the presentation of any A3s for metrics that are in the red. The monthly operating committee meeting is held, and at its completion, the functional leader brings back to the functional team members the messages from the committee meeting: CEO commentary, observations on company status as a result of all the Tracking Sheet reviews, adjustments that have been made to operations, and the company's business priorities going forward. The A3s are reviewed and discussed within the functional team, and members of the team understand the particular actions required to deliver on the agreed A3 action plan. This creates consistency of communication and alignment across all functions.

- **Week 4**: Continued meetings with the functional team to drive the priorities on the Tracking Sheet and from the A3s, as appropriate.

The Ultimate Effect of Your New Business Rhythm

The successful implementation of The Management System is a journey. There is no expectation of perfection, but it is essential for functional leaders to understand their function. So as companies implement the system, it is important for everyone to be patient. There will be challenges finding the source data for calculations that are required to support Tracking Sheet metrics. In some cases, the data simply won't be available in a company's existing information system. But there is a benefit to learning that. It helps companies understand what kind of data systems and IT infrastructure must be invested in and successfully implemented for the company to transform itself.

Enablement function metrics are particularly difficult to nail down. The companies we target with our investments typically do not have any formal enablement function capabilities in the company. Most of those functions are in the head of the founder or the CEO. But for a company to scale successfully, these enablement functions must be put in place and develop sufficient capability to keep the company growing. Additionally, because enablement functions such as strategy or product management have little impact on current year revenue metrics, these functions have limited value in a monthly operating committee review. However, they have significant value for the achievement of revenues in the future. For this reason, in the first year or so of the implementation of The Management System, I recommend that the operating committee meeting work the Functional Construct backward, from execution functions back to enablement functions. In almost every case early on, the metrics for the execution functions are much better understood in the early days of the implementation of The Management System and are easier to calculate. So a best practice at that point is to start your operating committee Tracking Sheet review with the execution functions and work your way back to the enablement functions, such as strategy, and then move on to the supporting functions.

One of the most important aspects of The Management System is that people cannot hide within it. Functional leaders are responsible for delivering on the metrics in their Tracking Sheets. Every month at the operating committee meeting, they must report on the performance of their function against its metrics. Time and time again, I have seen executives who were seemingly competent in their functional leadership not be able to execute against defined and transparent metrics. As I pointed out earlier in the book, the compensation of the senior management team is all tied to True North. Everyone is paid their variable comp on the same objectives. Therefore, when you come to an operating committee meeting, if there's one function not delivering, it will become readily apparent as to why. Candidly, there are just some executives who are better at presenting and debate than they are at executing very specific objectives. Those leaders will be challenged to succeed in a company that uses The Management System correctly. Sorting these people out will be important early on, enabling the company to create the culture of execution that is critical to companies that are at a growth inflection point and looking to accelerate their transformation to growth.

The entire management team has debated and agreed to the metrics that represent the top ten performance requirements each function must deliver on in the company's pursuit of True North. I know there will be functions that think there are important metrics that did not land in their top ten. And I also know that they'll want to discuss those in the Tracking Sheet reviews. But they must stay focused. The only thing that cannot change in the course of a year implementing The Management System is True North. So if you look at a Tracking Sheet and don't like a metric or don't feel that a metric meets the criteria for being a top ten metric, either get it taken off or exchange it with another—but do not allow a functional leader to focus on more than ten. I guarantee you that if you pick the right ten for each of the functional areas, and the functions perform against those top ten, the only outcome possible is meeting or exceeding your True North objectives. The key to successful execution is focus. That focus produces alignment, and that alignment allows the organization to do the most important work and say no to less important work in the pursuit of True North. Success comes from focus and alignment across all the functions.

My QHP colleague Karol Jarzabek does a good job of summing up the benefits of the new business rhythm that The Management System establishes in a company:

> If you think about what happens at many companies, if a plan within a particular function is going sideways, they go into firefighting mode to address the problem. Someone is analyzing the problem in isolation, disconnected from the rest of the company. Each function goes in its own direction in these situations, making isolated decisions about what's important, what they have to address. The rhythm of business introduced by The Management System standardizes the flow of key activities. Everything is brought to the operating committee meeting, where you review the Tracking Sheets for every function together as a cross-functional team and get input and support around your problems from everyone on the team.

This becomes this cadence of activity and problem-solving, a standardized approach for middle management so that managers aren't operating in isolation. You meet as a team and discuss what's going on. After the operating committee meeting, everyone has their numbers, evaluates their aspect of business, starts performing mitigation activities, and starts working in the direction that everyone had deemed most important for the company. Everyone pulls together, like a cohesive rowing team that has more strokes in alignment and therefore operates the boat more efficiently and achieves greater speed.

As I said earlier, better teamwork and greater efficiency across functions are what turn a good company into a great one, and that is what the business rhythm established by The Management System makes possible. In the next chapter, I'll describe how this system can take your company to the next level of growth.

9

BUILDING A FRAMEWORK FOR NEXT-LEVEL GROWTH

The successful development of The Management System builds a foundation for growth. It facilitates the transformation of a company with great potential but low execution prowess into a company with great execution prowess, capable of reaching its full potential.

But there's more! The Management System enables the ongoing acceleration of growth, both from an organic perspective and from an inorganic perspective. Organically, the company continues to improve its processes and operational performance while enabling every team member to better understand how the business works and how to work most effectively within the business. Inorganically, the combination of the Roles and Responsibilities Sheets and Tracking Sheets establishes a system that can accelerate an acquisition or a new partnership. These tools enable new capabilities to be integrated into the business flow in an accelerated fashion, while at the same time making those new capabilities clearly understood by your existing employees and by new employees joining from another business entity.

I've long believed that the most important benefit of a successful deployment of The Management System is the expertise gained by employees of the company as they better understand how the work of the company is done and how to efficiently work across functions, which leverages *all* the talent in the company toward a common goal. It's been said that a company is only as good as its talent, and with the successful deployment of The Management System, you have the best chance to attract and retain the best talent and get the most out of every individual in your company.

Accelerating Growth and Realizing Full Potential

Let's break down the elements of The Management System and learn how each one is critical to the accelerated transformation of your company and to realizing its full potential.

STRATEGY

I love talking to a potential portfolio company about QHP making an investment in their future. In almost all cases, the people involved are enthusiastic about what they're capable of doing, about how successful they could be in their market. We ask them to talk about their vision for the future, and the opportunity they see excites them as operators and us as private equity investors. A fundamental aspect to a successful private equity investment is alignment on strategy. As we've discussed, in The Management System, this vision of the future is expressed in the From-To Chart. It is critical to achieve alignment between the investor and the company about where we collectively want to take the company.

It is equally important for management to share this document with all the employees in the company. There are multiple benefits that come from sharing the From-To Chart with the organization. You want your employees to have a passion for where the company is trying to go and to connect to that strategy professionally and personally. You want people on the team who are excited about your future and passionate about the journey to get there. Additionally, this chart will describe the road map for that journey. This road map will certainly include capabilities within the company that need to be enhanced or operationally improved upon, and it's also likely to require additional capabilities that are market adjacencies or solution enhancements.

The road map allows the enablement functions to get to work on vetting strategies, prioritizing, and evaluating business plans—plans that provide visibility into investments that need to be made to accelerate the growth of the company. I've always believed that if every employee in the organization is clear on the strategy and clear on how they can contribute to the execution of that strategy, you will have a very special company that is an exciting place to work.

VISION, MISSION, VALUES

Over the years, I have learned that there are two types of companies. The first is the kind of company that creates a vision, a mission, and a set of values. These things live on the company's website, but they don't live in the behavior of the people in the organization. I've seen these companies struggle in their markets because they struggle with talent acquisition and retention. This is because by not working according to their vision, mission, and values, they become a less desirable place to work.

The second kind of company lives their vision, mission, and values and continually invests in the culture of the company. They're intentional about the articulation of their vision, their mission, and their values. They live them through the behavior of every individual in the organization, and they're successful in their markets because they become known as a desirable place to work, attracting and retaining top talent.

Nick Dyer, CEO of Catalyst, feels strongly about the importance of having a well-defined culture in a company in order to succeed:

> I am a really strong advocate for a very explicit, intentional culture. And what I mean by that is that we know the kind of behaviors we need to see among our employees to drive the kind of internal and external engagement that makes us successful. We're a human capital company. It's a professional services organization that provides clinical trial support and leadership for our clients. Our mission is to design and execute better clinical trials, and we do that through our expert teams aligned with technology. But the human element of that interaction is *really* important. We can't have a strong customer service ethos and deep level of engagement if we don't have a very intentional culture. We did a lot of work around what we wanted our values and behaviors to be, and those values line up very neatly with the elements of The Management System.

Here is QHP's experience with our portfolio companies. The companies who invest the most time and energy into developing their vision, mission, and values tend to live by them. In turn, they attract the best talent, have phenomenal retention rates, and display tremendous execution prowess in meeting their goals month in and month out. The result: *everyone* is aligned with the achievement of True North.

SWOT ANALYSIS

During the off-site with the senior management team of a company, I lead a discussion about the current capabilities of the company. It is not surprising that when you get an expanded group of senior executives together for the first time and ask them to do this exercise, the perspective of the group is different than the perspective of the founders/CEO. I usually break the management team up into three or four separate groups and have them work on strengths, weaknesses, opportunities, and threats separately. Then I bring them all back together, have each group present what they've come up with, and then lead a discussion where they choose the top five in each of these categories.

It is important that you have an honest assessment of where you are today to ensure you have the capabilities to capitalize on your strategy and your annual True North goals. Particularly when you assess weaknesses and threats, you become informed about operational priorities that must be executed immediately. Two examples of this are a company's brand awareness in the marketplace and its go-to-market capability necessary to execute against the current and future opportunities. The senior management team must make an honest assessment of where the company is today, because the current capabilities lay the foundation for the work that lies ahead. While you can't do everything at once, the Functional Construct of the organization outlines where the work should be done to assess priorities and where decision-making responsibilities lie. This must be clarified so that the organization can be aligned around executing the right work.

FUNCTIONAL CONSTRUCT

I have talked a lot about the typical kind of company we invest in as we look for companies that have tremendous growth opportunities. They tend to be smaller companies managed by a few senior individuals, with the rest of the organization simply following their lead without an understanding of the company's direction or changes happening. The organizational dynamic is effectively "the priority of the moment," which creates tremendous dysfunction and disruption in the operation of the business. It certainly *doesn't* create passionate buy-in from all the employees or their commitment to whatever market opportunity the company is pursuing.

One of the most challenging aspects of the management off-site is the exercise where we work together to create the Functional Construct of the organization. Having an expanded group of senior management people now discussing how the work of the organization should be done is often very enlightening for top managers and the entire group. This is also where all the cheese gets moved for senior executives who are used to making lots of decisions across all the company's functions.

Achieving alignment around how the work of the organization is done across the enablement, execution, and supporting functions is critical to the successful deployment of The Management System. The company knows that things have to change if they're going to capitalize on their opportunity, and now they find themselves discussing the construct of a functional organization that will enable that opportunity to be achieved. Attaining agreement and alignment across the senior management team for the Functional Construct is the first step in the engagement of the middle management team in where a company is going in the future. And, as I said earlier in the book, the single most critical element common among the most successful companies is an engaged and aligned middle management team that takes the strategy of the organization and translates it to the execution of the company's work through its employee base. The exercise of establishing the Functional Construct is when the engagement of this middle management team begins, and it is critical to the success of building out the rest of The Management System.

ROLES AND RESPONSIBILITIES

Creating clarity about where the work is done and where the decisions of the organization can be made is the first step in building efficiency and effectiveness into the execution of the work of the business. As I've described, if there is a piece of work that is important to getting the company's work done, it must land on a Roles and Responsibilities Sheet, but never on two of them. During the management off-site, this is harder to achieve than one might think, but it is a necessary part of this process. Creating Roles and Responsibilities Sheets—where it is clear what work is being done in which function, which inputs each function requires to do that work, what you expect the outputs of that work to be, and what decisions everyone is comfortable with the function making unilaterally—creates the framework required for a company to accelerate its growth and maintain that acceleration.

Pro-ficiency CEO Mike Raymer talks about how defining the roles and responsibilities in this new framework immediately points to the talent gaps:

> By clearly delineating the functions and their specific responsibilities on the Roles and Responsibilities Sheets, you figure out the kind of talent you need to perform the work,

to accomplish the kind of growth you want. It helps you identify key hiring initiatives so quickly. We can clearly see that, well, everybody works over here, and nobody is doing this other thing. The whole team sees it and buys in to the importance of hiring the people needed. So then the team goes out and hires the people to get that work done.

Mike also points out that young, small companies usually have too many people doing too many things across functions and are also missing functions that will be essential to accelerating their growth. The Roles and Responsibilities Sheets, he points out, immediately expose where these problems are in an organization.

TRACKING SHEETS

A company that is in a period of accelerated growth must be intensely focused, and Tracking Sheets ensure that focus. Where there is a great market opportunity, there are many paths that could lead to taking advantage of that opportunity. One of the greatest aspects of The Management System is the ability to choose one clear path and say no to the others, knowing what you're not going to do and staying focused on what you've agreed and committed to doing. Creating an operational plan to achieve True North and having it expressed across every function via the top ten metrics enables you to stay focused. And if you've chosen the right metrics—meaning they are the most important and each function stays true to executing successfully against those metrics—then you've given your company every chance to not only meet but exceed your True North objectives.

Ron Scarboro, CFO at Azurity Pharmaceuticals, points out how useful Tracking Sheets were for bringing focus and enabling improvements at his company:

One of the great things that Tracking Sheets achieve is getting people doing the same thing at the same time, focusing on the essential work that needs to be done. That was really helpful, considering the breadth of activities I implemented in the eighteen months when I had to rationalize facilities and make operational improvements. Over those eighteen months, the Tracking Sheets, along with the A3s, established our rhythm of business. We got everyone focusing on the same goals at the same time, so we could incrementally measure process improvement and adjust processes as necessary.

As I've said many times, things are not always going to go according to plan, and Tracking Sheets enable the entire organization to understand how the company is performing and how resources need to be allocated to deal with both challenges and opportunities. Tracking Sheets are a factual and transparent representation of how the work of the organization is being performed across all functions. They enable a fundamental understanding of the company's performance and provide a framework that every functional executive can understand and from which they will continue to learn about where leverage and opportunity points exist within the company.

A3s

When I was a CEO and one of our operational metrics on a Tracking Sheet either went red or was forecasted to go red, I liked it very much when a functional leader created an A3 action plan to get that metric back on track and engaged with the entire operating team to put it into action. Using this approach eliminated those lengthy PowerPoint presentations for which I've expressed my disdain, and they were far more useful. The A3s eliminated the power of persuasion as a tool, which is very important when the rhetoric doesn't match the ability to execute. A3s create a common language that makes problem-solving and action-planning a collaborative and positive exercise. It engages appropriate team members of the management team and produces accelerated action toward the achievement of True North.

My fellow QHP Partner Matt Jenkins thinks that the ability to put the focus on the *right* problem makes the use of A3s particularly effective:

> A lot of people, even high performers, see a problem and immediately want to jump on it and fix it. The A3 forces the discipline of figuring out the *most important* problem, the *root* problem, that you're trying to solve. I sometimes work with companies that don't use The Management System and therefore don't have A3s, and I always find myself using the phrase that sums up what the A3 helps you uncover— "What problem are we trying to solve here?"—if I see that somebody is doing something political or has a hidden agenda or whose actions don't line up with what's needed to achieve a real business outcome. I always used that question to tease out what exactly they're trying to solve for. I carry the A3 approach with me into these other contexts because I think having clarity about what specific key problem you're trying to tackle is a way of poking through all the junk that can get in the way of accomplishing something meaningful.

To reiterate what I said at the beginning of this chapter, *things will go wrong!* This is part of business—part of life. What distinguishes companies that succeed is their ability to *see* when things are going wrong *and do something about it.* The Management System provides you with an "early warning system" that identifies problems as they arise as well as a great tool for defining those problems and laying out the actions that will solve them.

CONCLUSION
THE POWER OF THE MANAGEMENT SYSTEM

Just two weeks ago, I joined the first operating committee meeting of the company we most recently invested in. This company was founder-owned, and one of the founders remains the CEO. We completed our off-site about implementation of The Management System about six weeks prior to this first operating committee meeting. As we were wrapping up the end of the day, the CEO turned to me and said, "I have learned so much about my business today." For me, that is the greatest compliment I can get about the powerful effect of The Management System. And she wasn't the only one who had learned a lot about the business in that first operating committee meeting; so did every other executive who leads a function for her organization. For the first time in the history of the company, the entire senior management team could see everything going on in the company from end to end—the enablement functions, execution functions, and supporting functions all in one place, all connected, all working together to enable the company to perform at its best.

The secret sauce for making any company great is an enabled and engaged middle management team, a team that not only understands their own individual roles and responsibilities but, more importantly, understands how they can—and must—work across functions and stay focused on achieving the company's True North objectives. Cooperation, focus, and execution: those are the keys to a whole new level of success.

The Management System off-site is an extraordinary commitment by the management team of a company that is at a growth inflection point. But it is well worth their time to spend an entire week aligning on vision, mission, and values; on understanding the strengths, weaknesses, opportunities, and threats of the company as it exists today; on breaking down the work into functional components through the Functional Construct; on developing the Roles and Responsibilities Sheets so that everyone knows where the work is being done and who is responsible for it, establishing decision rights within each function (which empower functional executives to perform), and pinning down the important objectives for each function on the Tracking Sheets; and, finally, on establishing a common language for problem-solving with the A3s. Yes, that's a lot of work and a heck of a commitment, but the off-site is where we initiate the activities that will accelerate the company's transformation and growth.

"I learned a lot about my company today." Wow. What a humble statement for a founder/CEO to make. And as I think about this company twelve months from now, about how good they're going to be at performing their work in an efficient and effective way, at accelerating their value creation on their way to realizing the company's full potential, I appreciate how useful The Management System framework is for enabling companies to succeed. It is a highly rewarding system to work with.

But don't take my word for all of this. Listen to what folks from several different companies we work with have to say about the system.

At Misys Healthcare Systems, Ben Clark saw the increase in speed and effectiveness as The Management System was driven down into the organization:

> After the senior management team got their minds around The Management System, once they felt comfortable starting to cascade it into their organization—for example, to the level of the individual support person within the support function—we really started solving problems much more quickly. Everyone was communicating, everyone was collaborating, everyone started seeing it when their peers were performing well and they weren't, which encouraged them to do better. And all those dynamics contributed to everybody getting up to speed, quickly transforming the way they worked and, as a result, rapidly transforming the performance of the whole company.

Pro-ficiency CEO Mike Raymer talks about how the system makes his job easier:

> The Management System is totally liberating for a CEO if it's really embraced—and the CEO *must* embrace it if it's going to work for the company. The system makes it easier to hold your direct reports accountable. It creates a framework for collaboration across the entire organization. Some CEOs

might worry that it will take too long to implement, to really make the platform effective, but it's really not that long a time, and it's well worth the effort. It pays off over the long term by enabling faster manager reviews each month, a clearer definition of each function's critical areas of work and ability to focus on those areas, and quick identification of things you need to correct operationally within the business.

Nik Morton, COO of Catalyst Clinical Research, describes how the documentation created by The Management System enabled him to hit the ground running at a company that was using the system tools effectively:

> I joined Catalyst in April 2022, and on my first day I spent most of my time reviewing the key documents from The Management System: Roles and Responsibilities Sheets, Tracking Sheets, and A3s.
>
> The Roles and Responsibilities Sheets laid out each of the key functional departments within the company, what those departments were accountable for delivering, and how they interacted with other departments. So I was quickly aware of how the organization was structured and who was responsible for what.
>
> Then the Tracking Sheets provided me with the specific metrics that measured delivery by each department against their accountabilities. And that made it easy to track performance by department, month by month, for the year so far. It showed me with a simple green or red box whether that function was successfully performing against its top

ten metrics. There were some challenges there, and I was immediately made aware of them.

Finally, the A3s laid out in a very consistent fashion when there was a gap between target and performance, the root cause for missing the target, and the recommended course of action to get the metric back on target.

So *within my very first day* at Catalyst, I had all that important information, and I went into a series of meetings with the department heads the next day fully informed about where the company stood. It was a complete and very rapid education about my new company!

I'd like to make a few final comments on what a founder/CEO should expect as a result of the implementation of The Management System.

Everyone's role and the work they do will change to some degree from what they were doing before and how they were doing it, in order for them to operate effectively within The Management System framework. But in every case, the most significant changes happen to the founder/CEO, so I want to speak directly to that person. You have effectively been responsible for *everything*, making every significant decision (and sometimes not-so-significant ones) and providing oversight of the entire organization—and that is what has enabled your company's success up to this point. But if your company is to transform, you must transform as well. This can be very difficult, and as you go through this process, you must recognize that difficulty and be patient with your transformation. It takes time to understand how the company is going to work in a new way, and it will take some time to build the right management team, one that you can trust and that can get the job done.

Moby Kazmi, MD, President and Cofounder of Copilot, is very clear about the fact that there's an adjustment required for a leader used to making all the decisions—and is also very clear about the benefits of making that adjustment:

The first couple of months it was very difficult for me, because I had always made most of the decisions. Nothing important happened without it going across my desk first. And this was the first time where that wasn't happening. Basically, you're giving your child to someone else, and they're saying that you need to just trust them with it. So it was difficult.

But then, in the operating committee meetings, I started seeing the metrics—even metrics I hadn't seen before, because we had been all over the place and now it was condensed and well organized. So the anxiety that I had initially got better with each operating committee meeting.

I started seeing improved participation from our team members. I started seeing better internal communications between the departments. There was more efficiency, there was less waste, and then I just saw better, more consistent control of our processes. And I was seeing all that through The Management System tools and the metrics. And let me tell you, as long as the business is doing well—it's on track and we have a healthy pipeline—I'll be happy. Plus, my life is better now. I'm able to hang out with my kids more!

If you stick to your own commitment to the tenets of The Management System, you will find the change in the way your company operates extraordinarily liberating. The Management System gives a CEO clarity about how and where the work is being done, and the Tracking Sheets show how well the work is being performed, providing visibility into the operations of the entire company. This enables you to offload work to your managers, as opposed to doing it all yourself, while keeping tabs on performance via monthly reviews. It is important that you hire the right people to lead the company's functions. As I've said earlier in the book, if you have good people, the job will be easy, but if you don't, it will be difficult. *The CEO's job is about people and strategy*, and you can't work on strategy until you get the right people to help you plan and execute it.

One of the rules that guided me as I built management teams is what I call The Rule of Thirds, and I encourage you to think about this approach as you build a management team at your growth inflection point. Consider keeping a third of the managers who currently lead functions for their experience and expertise with what the company does. Consider having a third of your team be promoted into leadership positions, bringing to the senior management team leaders within the organization who are talented and committed, but for whom there hasn't been an opportunity for promotion. And finally, bring in a third of your management team from outside the organization, finding people who will bring experience and expertise that the organization does not have but desperately needs to grow the business. As these executives work with you to understand their roles and responsibilities, understand how to work together across functions, and take on full accountability and responsibility for the performance of their functions, you will be free to focus on opportunities of strategic importance for the company.

Our strategy at QHP is to partner with the management teams of companies we invest in. We like to say that we take "execution risk" in our investments, and the way we mitigate that risk is by working with management teams to implement The Management System because we know it works! An important benefit of this interaction between the management teams and our QHP team is that we learn a great deal about the company via the initial off-site meeting and from the monthly operating committee meetings, which one or more of our partners attend. This enables us to leverage our experience and expertise precisely where it's needed in an engaged and knowledgeable way, not as an organization overseeing the operation from afar.

QHP and our portfolio companies are aligned with a common objective: to realize the full potential of the company. We work *together* to implement The Management System, which is a key enabler on the journey to realizing the company's full potential. A successful implementation transfers the ownership of The Management System to the portfolio company, which adopts it, adapts to it, and manages it over time so that it works successfully for them. Though the process of system deployment is reasonably consistent across companies, every individual company tailors the system to their own specific needs so that it works most effectively for them.

One of the great benefits of deploying The Management System consistently across all our portfolio companies is that those companies can share what they learn with one another. We currently have eleven portfolio companies sharing their experiences and knowledge with one another. This also accelerates the adoption of The Management System for new portfolio companies as they onboard. I understand that the Lean 6 Sigma way of expressing this is: they all shamelessly steal ideas and experiences of success from one another, which continues to promote their success.

Through the true partnerships we form with portfolio companies, we align on the strategy for enabling a company to realize its full potential. To do that, those companies must transform themselves because within the current structure and operating processes, they are unable to scale. The Management System enables them to lay the foundation for transformation and subsequent scaling. It is often said that the fun is in the journey. And in my experience with our portfolio companies, this is true of the journey we share with them as they successfully deploy The Management System. But we and our companies also enjoy the results as well as the journey.

ABOUT THE AUTHOR

HAVING GROWN UP professionally in companies such as IBM, Siemens, and Kodak, Vern leveraged that twenty-year experience to develop The Management System as a first-time CEO at Misys Healthcare. With an outstanding outcome at Misys, The Management System became the framework for successful transformations he led at subsequent CEO roles at MedQuist, M*Modal, and Medfusion. At QHP Capital, The Management System has become the framework for portfolio investments to accelerate the value creation for each. Vern's experience in management and in transforming companies has become a critical element in the success of QHP investments and in the development of management teams.

In addition to his professional experiences, he has also been a board member of several significant healthcare systems and most recently was chair of the board at his alma mater, East Carolina University, and remains a passionate Pirate.

Vern has six daughters and three grandchildren, and he lives with his wife, Julie, in Wake Forest, North Carolina.

APPENDIX

Contents

From-To Chart Example

	From	To
Business Model	• 2M+ patients in the database • 14 languages supported • 29 countries supported • Phase 1-4 supported • 120+ conditions	• 15M+ patients in the database • All languages and countries supported • Focus on phases 1-4 clinical trials, medical device studies, registries, DCTs, surveys, and commercialized product studies • All conditions -> consider breaking up into therapeautic area specialities
Customers	• 40%+ concentration with 2 customers • 68% concentration with top 5 customers • 50%+ of revenue from large pharma	• Under 15% concentration from one customer • 25% of revenue from large pharma • 25% of revenue from biotech • 25% of revenue from medical device • 25% of revenue from other (registries, surveys, DCT, commercialized products)
Service Offerings & Market	• Single product (patient recruitment) • Addressing / could address adjacencies (patient engagement, retention, etc.) but not upselling / monetizing • Addressable market is pre-enrollment only	• Expansion into patient retention • Establish brand as a true SME/partner: protocol design, site selection, diversity plans • Expansion into in-person site support (our current bottleneck) • Establish brand as the leader in data analysis with custom data analysis solutions • Expansion into commercialization product studies (E-consent, registry and survey tools
Enablers (capabilities, processes, systems)	• Limited back-office technology • Lots of data sitting outside the existing platform • Limited sales organization • Limited corporate marketing	• Sophisticated tech stack to support processes (Monday.com), revenue (HubSpot, Salesforce) and EBITDA growth (NetSuite) • Enriched patient database • Explore AI, create a holistic data ecosystem connecting all functions
Financials	• $50M of Revenue • $20M of Adj. EBITDA • 45% Adj. EBITDA Margin • 81 Employees + 20 Contractors	• $210M+ revenue (42% CAGR) • $120M+ Adj. EBITDA (48% CAGR) • 56%+ Adj. EBITDA Margin • 350+ Employees, 100+ Contractors

Mission, Vision, and Values Example

Mission

Improving health outcomes by
connecting people with clinical
research, anytime, anywhere,
accessible to anyone.

Vision

Empowering patients everywhere
by providing safe, direct, and equal
access to clinical trials and
research studies.

Values

1. Excellence
   - Deliver to your full potential
   - Strive for high quality
   - Own the results
   - Commit to continuous improvement

2. Collaboration
   - Be respectful and listen to others perspective
   - Actively participate
   - Trust and empower each other
   - Be a team player

3. Innovation
   - Solutions-oriented
   - Courageous and bold
   - Always striving to improve
   - Thinking outside the box

4. Integrity
   - Doing the right thing
   - Valuing diversity of perspective
   - Be honest
   - Practice empathy

5. Humility
   - Be open to feedback
   - Team first mentality
   - Be authentic, be vulnerable
   - Celebrate your colleagues

SWOT Example

Strengths	**Weaknesses**
• Technology • Service orientated (white glove service) • Talented and diverse colleagues and culture • Results • Communication and adaptability	• Articulation of value proposition • Functional process optimization and decision-making • Giving things away for free • Fragmented, poorly leveraged internal data • Overlapping roles
Opportunities	**Threats**
• Global brand building—establish leadership position • Putting processes in place to scale • Broader services • Pricing • Database enrichment	• Changing digital marketing landscape (i.e. cost of media placement) • Changing privacy regulatory environment • Attractive market brings competitors • Brand reputation fragility • Clients taking services in-house

Functional Construct Example

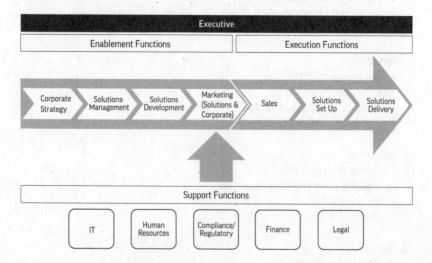

Roles and Responsibilities Examples

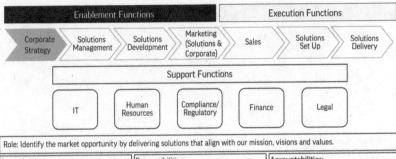

	Enablement Functions				Execution Functions		
Corporate Strategy	Solutions Management	Solutions Development	Marketing (Solutions & Corporate)	Sales	Solutions Set Up	Solutions Delivery	

Support Functions

IT	Human Resources	Compliance/ Regulatory	Finance	Legal

Role: Identify the market opportunity by delivering solutions that align with our mission, visions and values.

Dependencies:	Responsibilities:	Accountabilities:
• Corporate strategy revenue goals and positioning from the board • M&A strategy and sign off from the board • Data analytics from Solutions Development • Solutions modules and solutions module from Solutions Management • Voice of customer • Access to subject matter experts • Identify large strategic relationships from the board • FP&A reports from Finance	• Near- and long-term strategic planning • Prioritize strategic objectives • Perform thematic research • Produce business intelligence and insights • Understand current capabilities by utilizing feedback from Solutions Development • Survey market and competitive landscape • Continually evaluate of business market position via SWOT • Internal opportunity identification • Lead key company objectives • M&A analysis identification and execution • Maintain large strategic relationships and identify new opportunities • Build market cases and handover to Solutions Management	• Delivery of the strategic plan • Competitive analysis reporting • Organizational education on market trends, opportunities, challenges, etc. • Market opportunity and unmet need to provide to Solutions Management • Intel and insights to market drivers • Competitive impact assessment reports • Future partnership management • Strategic diligence assessment of an M&A target • Prioritize strategic objectives and opportunities

Major Decision Rights:
• Ranking methodology of strategy initiatives   • Analysis methodology
• Information sources

Skills Required:
• Business Strategy Development   • Market Research and Competitive Analysis   • Strategic Planning and Execution
• Financial Analysis and Modeling   • Mergers and Acquisitions (M&A) Analysis

Roles and Responsibilities *(continued)*

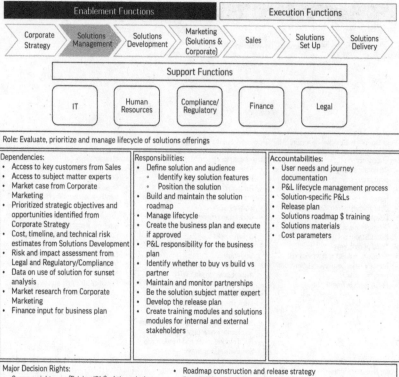

Enablement Functions					Execution Functions		
Corporate Strategy	Solutions Management	Solutions Development	Marketing (Solutions & Corporate)	Sales		Solutions Set Up	Solutions Delivery

Support Functions				
IT	Human Resources	Compliance/ Regulatory	Finance	Legal

Role: Evaluate, prioritize and manage lifecycle of solutions offerings

Dependencies:	Responsibilities:	Accountabilities:

• Access to key customers from Sales
• Access to subject matter experts
• Market case from Corporate Marketing
• Prioritized strategic objectives and opportunities identified from Corporate Strategy
• Cost, timeline, and technical risk estimates from Solutions Development
• Risk and impact assessment from Legal and Regulatory/Compliance
• Data on use of solution for sunset analysis
• Market research from Corporate Marketing
• Finance input for business plan
	• Define solution and audience
	  ∘ Identify key solution features
	  ∘ Position the solution
	• Build and maintain the solution roadmap
	• Manage lifecycle
	• Create the business plan and execute if approved
	• P&L responsibility for the business plan
	• Identify whether to buy vs build vs partner
	• Maintain and monitor partnerships
	• Be the solution subject matter expert
	• Develop the release plan
	• Create training modules and solutions modules for internal and external stakeholders
		• User needs and journey documentation
		• P&L lifecycle management process
		• Solution-specific P&Ls
		• Release plan
		• Solutions roadmap $ training
		• Solutions materials
		• Cost parameters

Major Decision Rights:
- Commercial terms (Pricing/GM) of the solution
- Strategic initiative go/no-go as relates to Solution
- Roadmap construction and release strategy
- Buy, build or partner
- Set solutions priorities for downstream functions

Skills Required:
- Business Plan Development
- Solutions management best practices
- Solutions development expertise
- Provided healthcare industry expertise and application
- Cutting edge technology and market knowledge

Tracking Sheet Examples

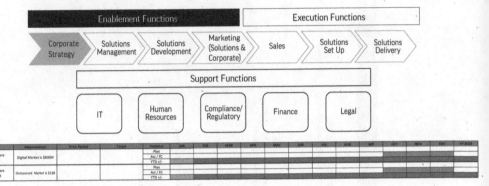

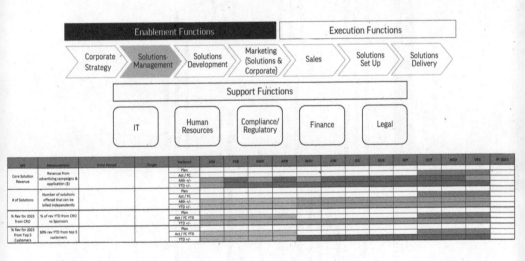

A3 Example

A3 Action Plan [October/2022]
EBITDA

Owner, Functional Area: [Finance]

Problem Statement – Performance/Gaps/Targets:
For October the Company missed the EBITDA target of 141K by 342K.

Goal:
Manage spending for the remainder of the quarter to achieve EBITDA.

Background:
Historically, the company's pipeline has been fed by the personal relationships of the founders and top executives without a structured marketing operation to drive market awareness, interest, and confidence in the company as a reliable, capable, trustworthy partner for large pieces of business. As the Company has continued to grow it has increased spending in areas such as recruiting, salary expenses, etc.

Root Cause Analysis: Why? Why? Why? Why? Why?
- Increased spending in key areas to increase business operations such as recruiting costs
- Fees associated with new audit, tax and valuation work.
- Investments in operational infrastructure (CTMS System, Marketing and sales software)
- Revenue was slightly behind targets

Recommendations:
- Bring new recruiting staff up to speed to reduce reliance on external recruiters
- Initial upfront investments in systems and initiatives should bring future cost savings and/or additional revenue
- Continue to build finance systems and forecasting to better forecast and manage spend.

OBJECTIVE	SPECIFIC METRIC	DATE	RESPONSIBLE
Create robust budgeting and forecast process to manage spend	Drive to direct margin % Manage SG&A spend as a percentage of revenue to target	12/19/2022	Tony
Complete 606 revenue project	Revenue implementation memo 606 Revenue adjustment for audit Revenue forecasting targets	1/31/2023	Tony/Kc
Develop ERP implementation plan	System selected Plan is in place Implementation partner selected	3/31/2023	Kc

Follow-Up / Unresolved Issues:
- Set meetings with potential implementation partners
- Schedule contract review meetings

A3 Example

Owner, Functional Area: Delivery

A3 Action Plan October 2022
Employee Utilization Under Target

Problem Statement – Performance/Gaps/Targets:
Utilization is currently at 83%. Target is 85%. Includes line management time. Billable employees are spending excess time on non billable activities or, in some cases, not coding time properly. Better visibility, analysis, management and accountability needed to achieve target. Utilization directly impacts True North as we could potentially take on additional work without the need to hire staff.

Goal:
To increase utilization to 85%+

Background:
Prior to June 2022 (later for some depts) visibility into employee utilization was lacking, contributing to inaccurate resourcing in some cases. Since then, we have:
- Worked closer with BD to scope FTE more accurately during the proposal stage
- Reviewed actual time spent with PDs and adjusted resourcing where needed
- Recently implemented timesheet entry and a process, adjusting and improving each week (need additional months of metrics to be certain)
- Low utilization leads to uneven distribution of work and decreased motivation; can also lead to a delay in resourcing studies, over hiring and potentially unnecessarily passing on change orders to clients

Root Cause Analysis: Why? Why? Why? Why? Why?
1. Staff are not completing time sheets correctly
- Bill codes are not always accurate in the new (learning curve) Harvest system: billable vs non billable; some tasks need to be more specific; Harvest not always ideal, HelpDesk not supportive
2. Studies are inaccurately resourced
- Study delays – Varying reasons: funding, IP delay, vendor delay, most often outside of Lexitas control – this leads to non billable time coded, with delayed project assignments frequently held– sponsors are unclear how long delay may last
- Inaccurate FTE scope in proposal – Scope based on minimal details from sponsor, major study changes before start up, unexpected effort needed for vendor management – projects awarded, team assigned, work started prior to final protocol (typical)

Recommendations:
- All roles/employees under delivery must be involved and accountable
- PTO to be pulled out, currently included in system report
- Better visibility, analysis, management and accountability needed to achieve target
- Flag employees under 85%, drill into codes/hours billed, frequency, LM/CSM follow-up
- Compile list of employees with bandwidth
- Ensure all depts/managers understand utilization and are coding their time properly
- Other CROs often have a more defined time per task allocation in the budget, allowing tighter management in this area. They also often have a separate resource to manage time tracking and resourcing.
- Relabel bill codes accurately and more specifically

Action Plan:
- Drill down into individuals at less than 40 hours and/or less than 85% billable.
  - Adjust codes/timesheets if incorrect
  - Update resourcing/availability if work can be added to employee
- Ensure all employees are in the system and compliant with time entry

OBJECTIVE	SPECIFIC METRIC	DATE	RESPONSIBLE
Continue reviewing each weekly submission – in depth review of less than 85%		30Nov22	Nicole/LMs
Follow up with LMs and project teams accordingly to resolve		06Dec22	Nicole/LMs
Adjust time codes/timesheets as needed/requested		09Dec22	Employee
Adjust resourcing if employee is under resourced – updated study assignment or help with billable tasks in interim		16Dec22	Nicole
Work with Sales/BD on process to review proposal/costing with PDs/Clinical Leadership for more accurate costing/FTE scope		16Dec22/ Ongoing	Nicole/BD
Add utilization to mid-year/year-end review for accountability		Jan 2023	Line Management

Follow-Up / Unresolved Issues:
- September and October began analysis by department
  - Sep ClinOps = 85%, Stats = 85%, ClinDev = 52% and DM = 71%
  - Oct ClinOps = 84%, Stats = 88%, ClinDev = 60% and DM = 77%

CONTACT

VERN DAVENPORT is a founding partner in QHP Capital, a Research Triangle, North Carolina–based private equity firm. QHP invests in growth-oriented life sciences services and technology companies. Vern's primary role at QHP is helping those companies scale and reach their full potential using The Management System as the framework to do so. Vern lives in Wake Forest, North Carolina, and you can find him at QHPCapital.com and on Instagram (@verndavenport).